DIAMONDS
in the
COAL DUST

DIAMONDS
in the
COAL DUST

Maddy
WORTH

ATHENA PRESS
LONDON

DIAMONDS IN THE COAL DUST
Copyright © Maddy Worth 2008

All Rights Reserved

No part of this book may be reproduced in any form
by photocopying or by any electronic or mechanical means,
including information storage or retrieval systems,
without permission in writing from both the copyright
owner and the publisher of this book.

ISBN: 978 1 84748 316 4

First published 2008 by
ATHENA PRESS
Queen's House, 2 Holly Road
Twickenham TW1 4EG
United Kingdom

Printed for Athena Press

Chapter One

It felt so good, even though the new shoes pinched a bit. Shuffling through piles of dead leaves, one hand held by Grandma and the other by my father, with my Mickey Mouse gas mask in a box over my shoulder, I was going to a new life.

Placed in a children's home at three years of age, life had not been easy, but today was special. I looked up in awe at the huge trees which were shedding their leaves to make the carpet which I was walking on. I didn't speak or ask questions. All I knew was that I was free from the constraints of the formidable Home.

One hour's journey later, we arrived at a strange house, where I was introduced to a lady whom I had never seen before. She was a kindly looking lady who spoke quietly. After a short conversation, Grandma and Father walked out without a backward glance and I was left alone with my new 'Aunty'. The first chapter of my life had ended. I was now an evacuee. I didn't cry.

How I came to be in the Home, a place primarily for orphans, of which I obviously was not one, I never fully understood. Snatches of information were gleaned over the years, but no explanation was ever given to me, save that my parents had split up and that nobody in my family – which was quite extensive – seemed to want to offer a home to a little three-year-old. I am sure there were reasons, but they were never explained to me.

In 1941, such institutions as the Children's Home were closed down in cities, as it was thought there might be a danger of German bombs dropping and causing damage. I did not remember much about the Home except for the biting cold and washing the floors on my hands and knees in a long line with the other children. It was later discovered, as Aunty undressed me for bed, that my feet were raw with chilblains caused probably by my not wearing socks in the extreme cold. I was later taken to the local doctor, who was horrified on seeing the condition of my feet. He was all for reporting the nurses at the Home, but as the place was already closed down, he probably thought it would be pointless.

I was a quiet, serious child, almost to the point of withdrawal. I hardly ever smiled, and had probably learned at an early age that it was pointless to cry or complain.

I quickly settled in with my new family, anxious not to do anything which might mean I would be sent back to where I had come from. Aunty was a kind and loving lady, a member of the Methodist Church, and also a member of the Air Raid Precautions, which sprang into action whenever the air-raid siren sounded. To a four-year-old child, it was quite exciting. I would be taken to the air-raid shelter in the care of a neighbour, as Aunty had to go round the houses in our vicinity to check that there were no lights left on, which presumably would alert any German bombers that might be flying overhead. Our village was in quite close proximity to several power stations, which were an obvious target for enemy planes.

The air-raid shelter was an awesome place. Set in the wall of an old quarry, it was dark and smelled very damp. Everyone would file in and sit on narrow wooden seats, sometimes for several hours, and wait for the 'all clear' siren. Most children, with the innocence of youth – not being aware of the possible danger – would sleep blissfully through the whole proceedings. I remember snuggling down in a clothes basket, oblivious to most of what was going on.

I had been with my new family just a few months, and one sunny Sunday afternoon had been taken on a country walk. I loved walking through the woods, looking up at the tall, leafy trees. On the way home, we stopped at a pub, and sat outside in the sunshine drinking lemonade, or a glass of beer in Uncle's case. It was a lovely day. Continuing our journey home, my legs suddenly refused to carry me and Uncle had to carry me the rest of the way. I was put straight to bed, but the next morning it was obvious that all was not well. The family doctor was called out and diagnosed kidney failure. I was put on a special diet and had to have complete bed rest – not that I could have got up if I had wanted to.

Diamonds in the Coal Dust

I had to be carried up to bed every night and downstairs each morning. Two or three weeks later, when I was beginning to feel a little better, a pram was borrowed – one of the large ones with springs – to take me out for a breath of fresh air. I suppose it was a strange sight: a child, obviously not a baby, perched on this huge pram; I felt so embarrassed. I was already something of a curiosity in the little village where everyone seemed to be related to each other.

The months passed, and I started school at the age of four and a half. I loved learning and was an avid reader. The teachers took to me, but I didn't find making friends easy.

My father was supposed to contribute to my upkeep, but didn't, and, as my aunt and uncle were rather poor, it was quite a struggle keeping me tidy and reasonably well clothed. Now and again, my aunt would take me on a journey which involved two bus rides – one to Leeds and then one out to the suburbs where my father lived with his parents and his new wife. My grandparents always made quite a fuss of me, Grandpa calling me 'fairy' and always giving me a handful of Nuttals Mintoes before I came away. This was a real treat, as everything was on ration at that time, especially sweets. Sometimes my aunt would strike it lucky and my father would provide the money for a new pair of shoes for me, but mostly she would have a wasted journey. Of course, at that time it did not seem very important to me – it wasn't until much later that I realised how unfair it was to my aunt, who struggled to make ends meet.

School was never an ordeal for me; I loved it. From my first teacher, Miss Foley, who would reward correct answers with a date cut from a block – no sweets in those days – right up to the headmaster by the name of Mr Hillcoat. Second class was taught by Mrs Brier who was a little awe-inspiring and always smelled of face powder. She taught the times tables parrot-fashion, starting with your two-times table. You were not allowed to move on to your three-times table until you could recite your twos perfectly – a practice never forgotten.

The next class was taken by Mrs Lunn, who never had a hair out of place. It almost looked like a wig! When she talked, spittle would form at the corners of her mouth, so that if you had to answer a question, you would be distracted and find yourself talking to her mouth.

The one teacher with whom I could not strike up any accord was the next one up. Mr Mitchell, the history teacher, was a strange, cold, distant man who used to come to school on a motorcycle. His helmet was leather and round – a little like a German soldier's helmet. His nose was red and shiny, and when he did speak to me, I found my eyes drawn to his nose, which was quite disconcerting for me. Thinking about it, it probably was for him, too! Even at that early age, I felt uncomfortable in his presence to such an extent that I took no useful part in any history lesson. As a consequence, history was my worst subject, a situation which stayed with me throughout my school life, even though subsequent history teachers were much more pleasant.

Mr Hillcoat, the headmaster, took us for reading and art. His favourite mantra was 'read, mark, learn and inwardly digest'. The reading was not a problem, as I would read anything I could get my hands on, but painting was a different subject altogether. I would begin a picture with a wide splodge of deep blue across the top of the paper – that was my sky – and another band of green was the grass, with a few colours dotted about for flowers. Mr Hillcoat would move around the classroom and as he would approach my desk my heart would start pounding nervously. He would take up a glass of water, whisk a paint brush around in it, then without squeezing it out he would drag the wet brush across my bright-blue sky. I would look at him in horror – what was he doing? – but the effect was magic. After loads of water and brushing, it actually looked something like sky. He was such a nice man, with a kindly manner, but, bless him, when I left junior school my painted figures still looked as though they had coathangers in their jackets.

When I first became an evacuee, I attended the Methodist Sunday school, as my aunt was a member. Each time I went to Sunday school, I received a star in an album. Once a year, we had a prize-giving day, where pupils would receive a book as a reward for attending regularly. It would usually be Whitsuntide, and the children would go with their new Whitsuntide clothes on. In the chapel, there would be a tiered stage and the older children would

Diamonds in the Coal Dust

file in first and make their way up to the top tier, with the younger ones filling up the tiers in between and the tiny tots on the bottom step.

It was a tradition that the children learned a little recitation to perform before their parents as a prelude to the giving of the prizes. Some of the pieces were quite lengthy, but the tinies had to be persuaded to say even just a couple of lines. The favourite piece for tinies was: 'I'm only a little girl, I've never been here before, but if I come again I will tell you something more.' Sometimes the recitor would manage to get through their piece before bursting into tears; sometimes the tears would come halfway through their performance and they would have to be rescued by a parent. This would be followed by the obligatory 'Ah'.

I loved singing hymns, and to this day can remember the words that my aunt used to sing to me. One of my favourite ones was a little verse that I have never seen in any hymn book:

> He's very old and weary – his aged head bent low.
> Into the old cathedral he sees the people go,
> And as he sits there and listens, the organ softly plays,
> He hears the prayer that his mother taught in childhood days,
> In childhood days.
> Lord, we are as little children, at Thy guiding hand we wait,
> Lead us ever through the darkness on to Heaven's gate.
> Glory be to the Father in Heaven above.
> Glory be to the Father of peace and love.
> Lift up your hearts to the cross of His tender care.
> Unto Him – unto the Lord – unto the Lord in prayer.

Gradually the chapel did not seem so popular with young ones and I began to attend the village church. I loved the atmosphere and the smell of incense as the leading member of the choir swung it back and forth, as the choirboys walked slowly down the aisle.

Sundays always followed a pattern. First, I went to Sunday school dressed in my Sunday best. Then, with a couple of friends,

Maddy Worth

I would walk from the church down into the village where I lived, up the steps to the top floor of the Miners' Institute. One could hear the 'oompah oompah' of several brass instruments. This was the meeting place for the local brass band's weekly practice. Uncle played the cornet, an instrument which was suited to his stature, as he was a slightly built man. I would take a seat at the back of the room and sit mesmerised by the variety and size of the instruments. Some of them, which the players seemed to wrap around their bodies, were enormous. All the men were elderly. Most of them had bushy moustaches which were tinted a ginger shade, apparently by the cigarettes or pipes which they smoked incessantly, as was the habit in those days. There was lots of puffing and blowing of musical instruments, interrupted at intervals by the tapping of the conductor's baton as an indication that someone had blown a wrong note.

After band practice, it was off to the allotment for a cabbage or cauliflower for Sunday dinner. I was sent home with the vegetables, while Uncle went off to the pub, where he would stay until chucking-out time. He would stagger home to a dinner that was hours past its best. Then he would become extremely abusive, using words I didn't know the meaning of and punching Aunty all over the place. She never said a word and neither did I. My silent anger was directed at my aunt for not saying something back or retaliating in some way against this obnoxious little man. I didn't realise my anger towards my aunt was unreasonable.

After his rage was spent, he would go to bed and stay there until it was time for the pub to open in the evening. I really didn't like him much at all. I used to think that if Hitler had ever come to our little village and heard Uncle's colourful language, he would have turned tail and run.

I clearly remember the day the war ended. I was on my way to the shop for my aunt when I met up with a girl I went to school with. She was wearing a very large red, white and blue rosette. 'It's over; the war's over!' she shouted. The shopping forgotten, I ran back home to relay the momentous news to my aunt.

In those days, there was no television and the radio was confined to an hour in the evening. The excitement was carried along the streets even though small children were not aware of the

Diamonds in the Coal Dust

importance of it all. Suddenly everyone was filled with euphoria; we could all begin to live again.

I, of course, did not remember life before the war began, but the enormity of the occasion brought such gladness to everyone that the whole village wore a smile. I supposed that now there would be no more queuing up at the little wooden greengrocer's shop for hours when a rumour flew round the village that there would be a delivery of oranges or bananas some time that day. Still, even that in itself was very exciting, especially if you managed to get papers on your oranges. The papers would be straightened out and hung behind the toilet door – so much more comfortable than newspaper, and perfumed.

The greengrocer's shop was owned by a man called John Patrick, a big man who wore a waistcoat which stretched over his ample girth, the buttons straining so much that if one of them had popped it would probably have put your eye out.

Another exciting follow-up was the removal of the miles of brown sticky tape which criss-crossed every pane of glass in the windows of most houses. This had been a protection from the dangers of glass shards, as windows might have shattered if a bomb had dropped nearby. The blackout curtains, which had been hung in the windows to shut out every chink of light, were eagerly ripped down. Things were slowly coming to life, and life was getting back to some normality. Of course, food and clothes were still rationed and would remain so for some time – for there could be no magic wand, no overnight miracle – but nevertheless there was a strength of purpose and an uplifting of spirits which couldn't be disguised.

Normal village festivities, which had been suspended during the war years, were able to be celebrated once again. Annually, there was a Joss wedding, which was a fair led by a horse and trap carrying a bride and groom, but there was a slight difference – the bride was a man and the groom was a lady. Then there followed a brass band and a procession of people in fancy dress. This parade of people made its way through the streets, ending up on the recreation ground, where there would be a fair to add to the festivities. Of course, the sun shone.

Several houses in the village had a mini shop in their front room – only on a small scale, of course – where one could buy five Woodbines or a bar of carbolic soap or some razor blades. One of the houses in the same street as mine had a bit of a clean-out and came across a box of balloons. These were handed out to the kids nearby, who had never seen a balloon before but soon got the hang of blowing them up, only to find that they were full of hundreds of holes where the rubber had perished with age. Still, it was fun.

Another exciting event was when old Fred would kill one of the pigs which he kept on the allotment behind the houses. Nobody saw the killing, but he would bring the lifeless pig on luggage wheels which were borrowed from the railway station. By the time the pig arrived, Fred's wife would have the copper boiler going to provide plenty of hot water for the job in hand. The children who lived nearby would gather round, me among them, and each jugful of boiling water that was poured on would make the pig seem to squeal. All the children would scream and jump back several paces, but they were assured that the pig really was dead and that it was just nerves that were making it squeal. I was not convinced.

Fred had a scraper which he used to scrape the bristles off the pig after pouring boiling water on to the carcass. After all the bristles were removed, a sharp knife was used to open the belly. This was when the girl spectators would take several steps back and the boys would push forward in anticipation. Shortly, one of them would be rewarded by receiving the coveted bladder of the pig. This would provide a few hours' fun as a good substitute for a football.

There was not a wealth of toys at that time, so children amused themselves as best they could. Empty treacle tins were washed out and would have holes pierced in the sides for string to be threaded through. Using the string as handles, you could walk on the tins like stilts. Every boy worth his salt had a trolley made out of any old pieces of wood and old pram wheels. Some pram wheels were purloined even before the pram was finished with! Where I lived, most of the children my age were boys, but that was not important, as all the games were unisex and played at an age when the segregation of gender was not important.

Diamonds in the Coal Dust

The outside toilets of most houses were situated across the yards and were housed in buildings where two toilets, side by side, were separated by individual doors. After dark, it was quite scary and one needed a torch to light the way. One of the games played was 'Run Sheep': this was where someone had to be the catcher and everyone else had to hide. One evening, I was one of the hiders and hid in the passage of the two toilets. It was very quiet, but not for long. Suddenly I was terrified by a loud yell of 'Gerrout!' I had done the unforgivable of disturbing someone on the throne, going about his business. I didn't need to be told twice, and never hid in such a place again.

Around the age of eight, I went through the dancing-class phase, so much so that I tip-tapped my way through shoes at a fair rate. One of the girls, who was a little older than me, used to try to organise us into performing concert material. She was a lovely girl who, unlike other older girls, didn't mind mixing with the younger ones. She would make bows out of crepe paper and fasten them onto our shoes and in our hair. We all thought we were the bee's knees. Sadly, the dancing classes didn't last long, as they had to be paid for and my aunt's resources were already stretched enough.

Once a week, I would be sent to the fish and chip shop to get a fish for Uncle and a penn'orth of chips for my aunt and me. It was a real treat. There would always be a queue right round the shop, though, and woe betide you if you were behind Minerva in the queue. Minerva was one of the characters of the village. She was a little bit 'not quite right', but she used to go to the fish shop for half the village. She would have a pocketful of orders on little bits of paper. If you were behind her, you knew you were in for a long wait. But everybody good-naturedly waited their turn without complaint.

Our milkman, a little man with shiny leather gaiters, would come round daily in a horse and trap with the big metal milk churns sitting in the back of the cart. Two jugs would hang inside the churns on metal hooks – one measured a pint and the other a gill, which was half a pint. You would supply your own jug and he would ladle the milk into it. It tasted so creamy and sweet, and, if it was left to stand, the cream would settle on the top. In later years, after the horse and trap became outdated, you could buy plastic dockets from the co-op – black or red, depending on whether you needed a pint of milk or half a pint. These dockets would be left on the doorstep where a milkman would come along in a milk float and leave the required milk. It was not half as interesting as the horse and trap, and the milk never quite tasted the same from a bottle.

On Sunday afternoons, an Italian named Curotto would come round the villages on a motorbike with a sidecar to sell the most gorgeous ice cream. Children would run out into the street to queue up for a cornet or an ice cream sandwich, which was ice cream between two wafers. Usually, I was sent with a basin and would ask for two or three scoops of ice cream to be put in it, which would then be served with either jelly or tinned fruit for a Sunday teatime treat.

In our village, we had a recreation ground (to give it its Sunday-best name). It was the hub of any village event, but the playing equipment had seen better days. I loved to hang on the swing, laying my head back as I swung higher and higher. I would imagine that the ground was the sky and the sky was the ground and the white clouds were fluffy pillows to walk on. There was a long slide, but towards the bottom the pieces of metal had come apart, so if you didn't jump off before you reached that part you ended up with torn knickers and a scratched bum. Not nice!

When I first arrived in the village, I spoke properly, if not poshly, but I soon learned to speak like the other children so as not to be singled out as 'different'. After a couple of years, I could say 'are yer offt ter rec?' with the best of them, rather than 'are you going to the recreation ground?' I don't think my aunt was too pleased with my new-found language skills. She would often tut-tut at me and say, 'You used to speak so nicely.' But I had to try to be just one of the village kids.

There were two cobblers in the village. In those days, shoes had to last until you grew out of them, and longer than that sometimes. It was fascinating to see the strips of leather being cut to the shape of a sole or heel. And the smell! I can still remember it now.

There was also a butcher's shop with sawdust on the floor. I

Diamonds in the Coal Dust

hated that shop, with the blood and the sickly smell of dead meat. That was one errand I hated going on.

The little corner shops were a revelation. There was no packaging as there is today, so you would get a mix of aromas: cheese, bread, biscuits, earthy potatoes (not the sterilised, super-washed ones that one buys today). The biscuits used to be kept in rows of tins, lined up and leaning forwards so that one could lift up the glass lids and help oneself to an assortment or a particular favourite, placing them into a bag which the shopkeeper would provide. One of the daring bits of cheek that the children liked to risk was to enquire if the shopkeeper had any broken biscuits – which were usually sold cheaply. If the proprietor said that he had, then the cheeky monkeys would say, 'We'll mend them.'

While I was at the junior school, my aunt's mother, who lived in a nearby village, became quite ill, so my aunt had to go and stay there and look after her. During that time, I had to attend the local school, which I found very enjoyable. The atmosphere there was much more laid back, as it was a very small school. One day, the teacher announced that anybody who had a pet could bring it to school the next day. I didn't have a pet, so I took a teddy bear. I will never forget the lovely chaos of that day, as over-friendly dogs dragged their little owners around in order to get nearer to the not-so-friendly cats. What a lovely, happy day.

The village had a maypole in the village square, which was taken down every two years for repainting. It would then be re-erected on May Day, when there would be a gala and several of the smaller village girls would dance around the maypole, holding ribbons and weaving in and out of each other, plaiting and unplaiting the ribbons. They had spent many hours practising the intricate moves, and it was delightful to watch. Of course, the sun shone all day long.

Each morning, for breakfast, my aunt would make porridge in a big cast-iron pan on her mother's old cooking range. I would get a spoonful of treacle and let it run into the porridge, marking out the initial of my first name; how I loved it. The six weeks spent in that little village were very happy for me. Then my aunt's mother became well again and we returned to our village.

An old couple lived at the end of our street – they weren't

Maddy Worth

even elderly, they were ancient. Mrs Priest and Old Eli didn't get out much and, on Saturday mornings, I would go shopping for them. I don't know why they were known as Mrs Priest and Old Eli and not Mr and Mrs Priest, but that was how it was. She was a small lady who had difficulty walking. He was a big man, without being tall; his head was large and completely hairless, he had no eyelashes and his eyelids were pink. Each Saturday I would go to see what Mrs Priest needed, with strict instructions from my aunt not to take anything as a reward. Every week I would get into this little tussle, with Mrs Priest trying to give me a threepenny bit and me saying that I wasn't allowed. Sometimes she would manage to slip a coin into my pocket and I would feel so guilty. She would say that she would feel hurt if I didn't accept it.

One particular Saturday when I called, Mrs Priest put her finger to her lips with a 'shh, shh' and drew me into the house. She took me quietly upstairs and I tiptoed into the bedroom. On a flat bed lay Old Eli. His bald head looked white and even larger, and the hairless eyelids were now white and tightly shut. 'He won't hurt you,' said Mrs Priest. I gazed in a kind of fascination and awe at the still, quiet form. I didn't know whether I should say anything or not, so I didn't. Old Eli was the first dead person I had ever seen – but he wouldn't be the last.

My aunt was not a spiteful person, it just wasn't in her make-up, but just once there was an incident – when I was around seven years old – which I never forgot. It showed a slight peevishness which was totally out of character for her. A lady in our street was a beautiful hand-knitter. She was a frail lady and in fact died quite young. She used to knit beautiful bonnets for her little daughter in different-coloured wools. The back of the bonnet used to look like a spider's web. My aunt was not much of a knitter, but one winter she endeavoured to knit me a pair of mittens in bright red wool. I was so excited and thought she must really love me if she were to knit something just for me. One mitten was completed and the second one begun. They were the most beautiful things I had ever seen.

In our street, a neighbour (who was a bit outspoken) had for some reason had a bit of a spat with my aunt, and they weren't speaking to each other. She had two boys, one a little younger

Diamonds in the Coal Dust

than me and the other quite a bit younger. As the older boy's birthday approached, a party was planned and the boy's mother asked me to go. I told my aunt and she said she didn't think I should go, but left it up to me. Being a seven-year-old, of course I wanted to go. I didn't understand about betrayal, but I did pay a price. When I got home, instead of one and a half mittens, there was a large ball of red wool; the lovely mittens had been pulled out. I can still feel the disappointment as I write this and I feel sadness, too. I never did have anything knitted for me, and to me it would be a token of love to have something created just for you. The mitten episode was never mentioned, and I don't believe that my aunt knew that I was absolutely devastated for some time afterwards.

The mining community was a special breed and very close-knit. Every villager had a male member of their family who worked down the pit. It must have been a terrible environment: always dark, sometimes hot, sometimes cold and nearly always wet. The only light would come from lamps fastened on the front of the miners' pit helmets and from the lamps which every miner carried. There were no toilets and no rest room. Their refreshments (called 'snap') were carried on their belts in a metal tin.

Uncle used to take just two slices of bread and dripping, and a bottle of water. That would have to sustain him for the whole shift. He did say that it wasn't very pleasant eating anything in the atmosphere at the bottom of the pit, where the air was thick with coal dust and hands were black and stiff with the cold and the muck. Rats, which ran amok down the mine, were quite well fed with discarded crusts. The only parts of a miner not black when he ascended to the pit top at the end of his shift were the whites of his eyes.

Miners were old before their time, having spent eight hours daily on their knee pads, sometimes in water, hacking at the coal face with a pick. At the end of their shift, they would drag their weary bodies homeward. One could hear the clip-clop of their pit clogs, walking down Pit Lane in little groups and splitting up to go their separate ways when they reached the main road.

At our house, my aunt would be up and have the fire going to heat the water by the time Uncle arrived home. The tin bath would be lifted down from the kitchen wall and filled with hot water, ready for Uncle to climb into. I once woke very early one morning and, not knowing what time it was, went downstairs into the sitting room. I was amazed to see my uncle sitting in the tin bath in front of the fire. My aunt was bending over and pouring water from a ladling can over Uncle's shoulders. His back was jet black with coal dust, and as the water ran down it made pink rivulets on his back. She was almost lovingly swooshing the water over his shoulders, but she couldn't be, not with the way he treated her. My aunt must have become aware of me standing there, for she jumped up and shooed me back upstairs. I will never forget that scene.

It must have been very hard before pit baths came into being for both miners and their wives, who had the unenviable task of washing the cardboard-stiff pit clothes without the convenience of a washing machine. Who knows, perhaps the working conditions of my uncle were a factor in making him the person he was. Getting into a cage at the pit head with a gang of other miners and being dropped into the bowels of the earth must have seemed like hell, and could have accounted for the animal-like way he treated my aunt. That said, most of the miners that we knew were very nice men, and seemed to be good providers and loving fathers.

Most of Uncle's wages went to support the brewery or the local bookie. My aunt would try to make ends meet by doing a bit of charring (cleaning) and babysitting. But if Uncle had a win on the horses, she would get me to ask him if I could have a new dress or suchlike. Sometimes he would come up trumps, but my aunt never dared ask him herself. It was so sad and I did hate him at times.

If the pit was the heart of the village, the Miners' Institute was the soul. Downstairs was the engine room, where the drink and gossip was carried out. Upstairs was the function room, where band practices, meetings, social gatherings and dances were held.

Once every couple of months, a dance would take place and it was a truly wonderful occasion, particularly for the kids my age, as it was one of the rare nights that I was allowed to stay up late. In the middle of the ceiling hung a magnificent glitter ball, which turned slowly to reflect thousands of lights. It seemed magnificent to me as a child, but years later, looking at it with adult eyes, it seemed a bit tacky.

Everyone would be dressed in their finery, there would be a band playing, and there would be a buzz of excitement round the room. My aunt was quite a good dancer, so I knew all the steps to the veleta, the military two-step, the barn dance and the tango. However, I could never float round like some of the beautiful young ladies; how I wished that I could. It was strange that I was so heavy-footed, as apparently my mother had won prizes for dancing in her heyday. However, heavy-footed or not, I loved the dance and was always sad when it was over. As the dancers poured out onto the cold, dark streets, it was a safe bet that there would be at least one inert male laid at the side of the road. I used to whisper to my aunt, 'Is he dead?' 'No, he is only asleep,' she would reply. I thought it was a strange place to go to sleep. She never did say, 'No, he is blind drunk.'

My father's sister was a professional dressmaker – in fact, she had her own label. My aunt managed to acquire a nice piece of tweed and it was made up into a coat and skirt for me. I really thought I was the bee's knees walking out in my new finery, but that was a one-off. There weren't many such gestures from my father's family, and it was left to my aunt in the main to make sure I was kept tidy. I know now it was a mammoth struggle most of the time.

Another of my father's sisters would send me a *Rupert* annual without fail every Christmas, but that was the only contact I had during my childhood, even though she had no children of her own. During the war and for some time afterwards, toys were in short supply along with everything else, but on Christmas morning I would have my *Rupert* annual, an apple and orange, and probably some sweets. I would stay in bed until I had read my book from cover to cover.

School holidays were long, carefree and, for the most part, sunny. We made our own entertainment and needed nothing more than an empty jam jar, two slices of jam and bread, and a bottle of water. There was an instruction to be back before dark, nothing more. A posse of us would set off over the daisy banks, poking about in the little beck on the way to see if anything moved. We usually ended up at the pond and if it was the right time of year we would get frogspawn, sometimes tadpoles. We would take them home, where we would be told to get rid of them PDQ before they turned into frogs. Sometimes we would head off through the woods and gather hazelnuts or pick blackberries, which were greatly prized as they could be made into a lovely pie.

In the Christmas holidays, if it had been snowing, it was down to the daisy banks for sledging. I say sledging, but it was only the better-off kids who had a sledge. The rest of us would go down the hill on a) a shovel, b) a bit of corrugated tin or c) a piece of old board. So it isn't too hard to imagine the state I used to go home in sometimes – wet through, with no backside in my pants and very cold. But it was good fun.

In my childhood, there always seemed to be snow in winter and lots of sunshine in the summer. Fog was also a regular part of winter, real pea-soupers as they were called. As we lived in the end house of a terrace, our toilet was a little way off and stood on its own. I hated going at night, so didn't unless it was really necessary. However, one night I *had* to go, and took the little paraffin lamp to guide me. This offered no help at all in the thick murk of the fog. As soon as I left the safety of the house wall, I was in no-man's-land. I totally lost my bearings and was groping around, desperately trying to touch something solid to hold on to. I went round and round in circles with tears streaming down my face until a neighbour loomed up out of the gloom and guided me back home. I will never forget that feeling of helplessness and desperation.

I only met my mother once during my childhood, but I did have a faded photograph. She looked beautiful and I used to pretend that she was Margaret Lockwood, a famous film star of the era. My mother's name was also Margaret and I used to imagine that one day this film star would turn up at my house and say, 'I am your mother and I have come to take you home.'

The one time that I actually came face to face with her was a very strange experience. My mother's father came to visit me at my aunt's and asked if I could spend the weekend with him and my maternal grandma. I was a little apprehensive at going to stay with people I did not know.

On the second day of my visit, I was taken on a bus ride and arrived at a house that was divided into apartments. As we climbed the stairs to one of the apartments, the door opened and a lady came out. Of course, I recognised her from the photograph as my mother. We looked at each other; I didn't feel as though she was my mother. I believe she said 'hello', but there was no cuddle or any of the things that I thought mothers should do. I wasn't even sure what proper mothers did, but it was a very strange experience. I think it probably was for her, too. It was to be twenty years before I saw her again. She did actually look like Margaret Lockwood, with masses of dark hair and very elegant, but she was not a good mother.

There was a row of stone houses opposite ours; in fact, it was the street where Fred (the pigman) lived. Almost opposite our house lived an elderly couple with their two grown-up sons, one of whom was married. The younger son was seeing a young lady, and there was great excitement one day when it was learned that they had married and were to live with David's parents. Liz was like nobody I had ever seen before: very glamorous, with lots of make-up – she wore bright red lipstick – and piled-up hair. But the most impressive thing for me was her gramophone. She only seemed to have one record, however, and played it constantly. What David's mum thought of 'Twelve Street Rag' is anybody's guess, but it did get a bit boring eventually. As it happened, they did not live there very long, as they soon got a place of their own. Later on, Liz and I were to become good friends.

My aunt was quite keen on good manners and, even though my English had become quite broad, I was expected to show good manners at all times. 'Please' and 'thank you' came naturally, but I also had to have good table manners. My knife and fork had to be held correctly and laid neatly side by side when finished with. I had to ask to be excused from the table if I wanted to leave before everyone had finished. If I made the mistake of leaning on the table during mealtime, I would hear 'uncooked joints off the table, madam'. How times have changed.

At around the age of ten and a half, I heard about a scholarship at school, which didn't mean much at the time. But one day I was informed that I would be sitting an examination. The children who weren't sitting it were given the day off school. We had an exam in the morning and one in the afternoon. Nobody seemed particularly stressed; we had a lovely carefree lunch where all the tables were pushed together like a party. It seemed such fun, not at all stressful.

Some three months later, I was standing in the school playground waiting for the bell to ring when the headmaster came striding towards me. He wiggled his finger and beckoned me towards him. I was very nervous, but he was smiling. 'Go straight home and take this letter to your aunt,' he said. I didn't say a word, just turned and ran.

By the time I arrived home, I was totally out of breath, having passed several of the children who lived near me without stopping to reply to their 'where are you going?' I thrust the letter into the hand of my surprised aunt. My mouth was dry from nervousness and the fact that I had hardly drawn a breath all the way home.

She opened and read it. 'Well done,' she said. 'You have passed your scholarship.'

I took the form that my aunt signed and went back to school at a more sedate pace. Back at school, the names of the pupils who had won were read out in assembly. Everyone seemed pleased, especially the teachers; I wasn't so sure. I had a feeling that things would never be the same again. I had never been out of the village on my own before, and the trip to my new school would entail a forty-minute bus journey each day, there and back.

I did enjoy the shopping trips to buy the long list of items of school uniform. As my aunt was classed as being needy, she was eligible for a school grant, which was a big help towards the costs. It was still a struggle for her, as the list of things available on the school grant list did not cover everything, but it was a big help. Some things that were not considered essential, however, had to wait.

The first day at my new school arrived, and I thought I was the bee's knees. My gymslip and blazer were both brand new and my shoes had been polished so much I could almost see my face

Diamonds in the Coal Dust

in them. My new satchel was empty except for my new pencil case. On my head I had a beret – the choice on the uniform list was for either a beret or a hat, but the hats were so much more expensive that my aunt could not justify the extra expenditure, although my beret did have the school badge on. The badge motto – *possum si volo*, meaning 'I will if I can' – was worn proudly and had to be respected whenever it was worn, even out of school time.

The bus journey over, we were dropped off in the town and had to make our way up through the town to the school. The prefect on our bus acted as chaperone to the newcomers, for we were little compared to the sixth-formers, some of whom were nearly eighteen years of age. We walked in a long line, like a crocodile, weaving our way along in the same direction. The prefects were chosen from the elder pupils, and if a prefect saw a pupil not properly attired – such as being without your hat in town – then you were reported to appear before the headmistress the next morning. There was no chance of us first-years doing any such thing – at least, not in the first two years. As we grew older and more confident, we did push the boundaries a bit.

Our uniform was dark green with a gold badge. Our berets would be perched on our heads at a jaunty angle and the older we got, the jauntier the angle. How they stayed on our heads I will never know!

We had green gymslips, which buttoned on the shoulder and had three-inch hems, which were let down at regular intervals as legs grew longer. In winter, we wore black woollen long stockings, fastened with suspenders (no tights in those days). These were lovely and comfortable when they were new, but when they had been washed a few times they shrank and got shorter and shorter, so that the suspenders stretched to kingdom come. There was always the risk that as you were walking there would be a ping and the suspenders and stocking top would part company. It also influenced how you would walk – as the stockings became shorter, you would find yourself adopting a gait where you were almost bent double in order to prevent the suspender being overstretched. Sometimes, when we were out of sight of the school, we would roll our stockings down round our ankles and hope we wouldn't be spotted by the uniform police.

However, those joys were still to come as I arrived for my first shiny new day at my shiny new school. I was sick with nervousness and trepidation, and my first sight of the school did nothing to allay those fears. It was an old, forbidding building with pointed domes on the roof. After my little familiar village school, it was very scary. I followed the throng into the assembly hall where we were ushered into order of age. Newcomers were at the front of the dais, with lines of pupils going backwards in year until the sixth-formers brought up the rear.

The hall was huge, with pictures and achievement boards lining the walls, along with a roll of honour. The headmaster and all the teachers were seated on the platform and they made a very impressive sight with their long black gowns billowing out behind them. The headmaster addressed the gathered pupils, welcoming the newcomers and hoping that everyone would have a good and productive year. The first-years were told to stay behind after assembly to be allocated our form teacher and classroom. Thirty of us were allocated 1B, and we followed our designated teacher to the correct classroom. I didn't know a soul and still felt sick.

Register was taken, where we had to identify ourselves to the teacher as our names were called out. The boys were all called by their surname, which I thought was a bit rude, but apparently that was the normal procedure.

The first morning was taken up with making our timetable, and I was alarmed to realise that each subject had a different classroom. I was terrified of getting lost, which I did several times that first dreadful week.

At lunchtime, we were told to go to the hall, where there were lists of names and table numbers for the refectory. Scrutinising the lists with hundreds of names on them, I couldn't find mine anywhere. By this time I was the only one left in the great hall. I felt so desolate that I went to the toilets, shut the door and cried. What was I doing here? I hated it.

After three days of no lunch, I plucked up enough courage to knock on the door of the formidable Pat, who was in charge of the allocation of dining places. My knees were knocking as I gently tapped on his door, secretly hoping that he would not be in. 'Come,' a voice boomed. In I crawled like Oliver Twist asking for more and told him in a trembling voice that I couldn't find my name on the dining lists. This fearsome, huge man with his flowing gown, who had a frightening reputation, gently put his arm round me and guided me out into the hall. I gave him my name and form number and, after scanning the lists, he found the problem. 'Ah ha!' he said. 'There we are.' A girl in the third year with a name almost identical to mine had been allocated two places by mistake. He apologised profusely and escorted me to the dining hall, where lunch was in full swing. I perched on the end of a bench and said that I really was not very hungry anyway. I was so embarrassed and, being a newcomer, I wasn't aware at that time of the reputation that Pat had. Perhaps it was just as well!

Each day there was a teacher on duty at lunchtime at the door of the dining hall to check hands and nails. Most of the teachers did the task perfunctorily, but if the cry 'It's Pat' went up there would be a scramble for the washroom, especially by the boys. But I can only remember him with kindness for the way he treated me. He was the Latin teacher and as Latin was not in my curriculum I did not have any other contact with the infamous Pat.

I stumbled to half-term in a kind of dazed terror; I should have been enjoying my time there, but I wasn't. I was so shy and introverted that I didn't seem to make any meaningful contact with any of the other pupils. I felt like a fish out of water.

During my first year at grammar school, it was decided that perhaps it would be better if my uncle and aunt applied to adopt me. It was suggested that my father might want me back when I left school and started work. I wasn't particularly taken with the idea, especially when I learned I would have to go to court for the application. However, the day came and my aunt, uncle and I went to the local magistrate's court. Everything went through without a hitch and I was asked if I wanted my surname changed to that of my uncle and aunt. I said that I would prefer to keep my own name; I struggled with change of any kind. I was also told that I could call my aunt and uncle 'Mum and Dad', but I declined that suggestion as well. I felt I was struggling with my identity as it was, without further complications.

The next day, I had to take a letter to my teacher explaining why I had been absent the previous day. I was mortified to learn that the letter had been left open on the teacher's desk and there were whispers that I had been in court. Nobody asked me why, but there was much speculation. I felt like a criminal.

At the end of my first year, it was no surprise to learn that I had wasted the whole of it and I was moved down a grade. I was ashamed, but although it did not do anything for me academically I settled into my second year much more quickly. Knowing several of the pupils from my village who were in the same form, there was a little more camaraderie. I won't say I flourished as, to this day, I am ashamed to say that I wasted my time at grammar school, but I was much more comfortable if I could sit at the back of the class and be overlooked. It wasn't that I was lazy; I just felt I had been left so far behind that it was impossible to catch up.

My favourite subjects were English, French and German, but my aunt could not see what good French and German would be to me in my career. I was 'encouraged' to think about dropping German and taking up Commerce, which was shorthand and bookkeeping. How boring was that? I loved German, probably because it was one of the few subjects I was any good at, but my aunt thought that an office job was a decent job for a young lady.

During my second year at the school, my uncle became quite ill. He had suffered with his back for some time, as did most miners, but the time came when he could no longer work. He was treated for a slipped disc, lumbago, sciatica – all without any improvement – until it was eventually found out that it was much more serious.

He went to hospital for tests, and it was discovered that he had bowel cancer and nothing more could be done for him. He was sent home from hospital the week before Easter and was confined to bed. I kept out of the way as relatives came and went, but on the Saturday before Easter Sunday I was woken by my aunt and told to get dressed and come straight downstairs.

I sensed that it was serious, and on the way downstairs I peeped in and looked at Uncle. He looked as if he was asleep. My aunt asked me to take a note to Uncle's sister, who lived on the other side of the village. She came back with me without speaking.

Diamonds in the Coal Dust

This time there was much more activity in the house. I was told to make myself scarce. I didn't cry, but I didn't know where to go, so I just walked down the village street as far as the rec and back again. When I arrived at the house, it was very quiet. A neighbour was with my aunt and, of course, the teapot was out. One thing that never changed in our village was that whenever there was a 'situation', the teapot came out – a sort of cure for any of life's little troubles, and big ones, too. The strange thing about that day was that at no time did anybody say to me, 'Your uncle's died.' It's strange that Mrs Priest trusted me enough to take me to see Old Eli when he died.

The next day was Easter Sunday and, of course, I went to church as usual. When they began singing 'When I survey the wondrous cross' – that's when I cried. I don't know why. I suppose I realised that something had ended and nothing would be quite the same again. After the funeral, things became much more calm and peaceful. Of course, that wouldn't last.

My aunt had lived in the same stone-built, back-to-back house all her married life. There were ten houses down one side and ten down the back. My aunt's best friend lived in the house immediately behind us. If one of them was putting the kettle on, there would be a knock on the dividing wall and a shout of 'cup of tea nearly ready'. It would be the same with the neighbours in the adjoining house; a knock on the wall would bring someone at a moment's notice. If anyone baked, it would be shared, as nobody had very much in the war years, and indeed for several years after. One thing those houses did each have was a massive iron range with a huge coal fire, as most of the occupants were miners.

Some months after Uncle died, letters arrived stating that the houses were to be demolished and everyone would have to find alternative accommodation. This was a big shock as this little community had been together for many years.

My aunt found a little cottage in the centre of the village – very old, but it had a front and a back door, which we had not had before. The walls were crooked and the floors uneven, but it was a nice little place. Aunty bought some wallpaper and we set about making it a bit more homely. A friend of mine gave a hand as well, and we were quite pleased with our new home. My aunt was offered the chance to buy it for £25, which she did, so that she had no rent to pay.

For the next couple of years, life rumbled on. Probably the most exciting thing for me was having my hair chopped off. As a small child, I had masses of blonde curls, but as I grew older and my hair grew longer, it was scraped back into two plaits. I didn't have my hair cut for years and when it was brushed out it came below my bottom. The wife of the vicar was a hairdresser and ran a little hairdressing business in the vicarage. I had been asking my aunt for a while if I could have my hair cut, but she wasn't too keen on the idea. However, eventually she was persuaded, as long as I had just half of it cut off. I was so excited, and the freedom of being able to toss my hair about was unbelievable. It came to just below my shoulders and was very thick and wavy.

However, a little while later the fashion was for a shorter style – I believe it was called the 'Italian boy cut' – so that was what I finished up with. I felt so grown-up and free. Make-up came later.

School became less of an ordeal as friends were made from other villages and my circle of friends widened. Someone or other would be having a party and the same faces would be seen at each get-together. Sometimes two or three of us would have to walk several miles home, as transport to our village was not very good. But there was a mix of boys and girls, and the journey didn't seem so long, unless one of us had been daring and worn shoes with 'silly' heels, as my aunt would say. I mostly had to settle for sensible shoes.

In my last year at grammar school, we had to decide which direction our working life was going to take. Having been steered towards a clerical vocation, I turned up at Lewis's department store for an interview in the cash office. Going to the staff entrance and being directed towards the interview room was only slightly less intimidating than my first day at school. I was offered a job, but I don't think that was a wondrous feat, as I believe that the manageress was an old girl of the grammar school, so it was almost guaranteed that any ex-grammar-school girl who turned up for an interview was offered a position. My aunt was more pleased about the job than I was.

I went back to school until the end of term. It was a bit sad to say goodbye to the friends that I had made and also some of the teachers. It was the end of another era, but I had grown in strength in the last couple of years, and was more able to cope with whatever my new life threw at me.

Chapter Two

So, one Monday morning in September, I presented myself at the staff entrance, along with several other new starters, to 'clock in'. Then it was off to the cash office to report to the manageress. Two girls were selected to stay in the cash office, and the rest of us were taken to various booths which were situated one in each department. The manageress dropped a girl off at each booth. A float, which was a bag of loose change, was given to each girl. When a member of the sales staff sold an item, she would write a bill out for the amount of the object and present it with the cash. It was the job of the girl in the booth to stamp the bill and put the correct amount of cash in her drawer, giving the correct change where necessary. When the last customer had left, then the cashier's job was to take her bag of money to the cash office along with the bills. The money had to be counted and had to tally exactly with the bills of sale.

My job entailed working four and a half days in the booth and one day a week in the cash office. Saturday was a full day, with the half-day being worked on Wednesdays. By the time I had cashed up on Wednesday and caught my train home, it was almost teatime – not much of a half-day. There wasn't much chance of making friends in the environment I worked in. The cash booths were like coffins stood on end. I was let out for an hour at lunchtime, but apart from that the only contact I had with anybody was when they came to my booth with a bill. We were placed in a particular department for a week, so that every Monday we changed departments. If you were put on a quiet section, the time went very slowly.

The best part of the job was the train journey. There were usually three local girls and two boys travelling on the same train from our village. We would all pile into the same carriage (these were separate from each other), with two rows of bench seats

Diamonds in the Coal Dust

facing each other. You couldn't pass from one coach to another as there was no corridor. There was much jollity and teasing. If it was someone's birthday – especially if it was a girl – they would usually finish up on the luggage rack. Once, when I was going through my knitting phase, my ball of wool somehow got accidentally thrown out of the train window. It stretched the length of the train, flying in the breeze, with me reeling it in as fast as I could. The journey home was equally light-hearted.

As I had to stay to balance my money, I was usually running for the train, but one or other of my travelling companions would be looking out for me as I ran down the platform, holding the door open for me.

As I walked from the station to the store where I worked, I daily watched the progress of a new ladies' fashion store which was being built. It looked very grand. When it was nearing completion, a notice appeared in the window inviting people to apply for positions. I mentioned this to my aunt and said I would like to go. She didn't think it was a very good idea to change jobs so soon, and felt that I should stay in my present job a bit longer to get used to it. I stuck it out at the store, imprisoned in my kiosk, bored senseless for another month. By this time, the new store was open, and in my lunch hour I would go and look in the window. The girls and ladies working there looked so happy. So, cometh the hour, cometh the man, and one day I plucked up the courage to go inside and ask to see the manageress.

To my surprise, the receptionist got on the telephone and told the manageress that there was a young lady enquiring about a job. 'Young lady'! I suddenly felt very nervous, but there was no time. I was told to go upstairs to the second floor to the office of the manageress. I immediately fell in love with the small, platinum blonde, elegant lady. She was like nobody I had ever seen before. She was so sweet and immediately put me at ease. She asked me what I wanted to do, where I worked and why I wanted to leave. She told me she had a vacancy for a cashier bookkeeper and asked if I would be interested. I think I would probably have swept floors for her. She suggested that I tell my aunt and see what she thought. Before I came away, she knew almost the whole of my life story. She genuinely seemed interested in what I had to say, and it was arranged that I would call in to see her the next day when I had talked to my aunt. I couldn't wait for home time to come so that I could hopefully get my aunt's permission to leave Lewis's behind. She was a little surprised, but she said that if I was sure that it was what I wanted, then she was OK with it. I eagerly worked my week's notice, and looked forward to my new employment with an enthusiasm I hadn't felt for a long time.

The shop was quite exclusive, and sold very expensive gowns and other fashionable garments. It smelled delicious and the carpet was very luxurious. Everything was brand-spanking new.

My first day at the new job was more exciting than scary – with no clocking on, it was much more sedate. The lady on the door, who was a sort of female commissionaire, was dressed in a uniform a bit like a soldier's with brass buttons. If anyone needed to go up in the lift, she would press the buttons and escort them. She asked me if I wanted to go up in the lift, but I declined and climbed the stairs, over the plush carpet, through the glamorous showroom and up to the office, to be met by my manageress.

My cash desk was in the middle of the second floor. It was a modern square structure and I sat in the middle on a swivel office chair so that I could see on all four sides without standing. It was very comfortable and so different from the 'coffin' cash desks at my previous place. I actually felt like part of the workforce.

The hierarchy in the showroom was very structured and not negotiable. The First Sales got the first customer who needed attending to, and so got the first chance of a sale. So if just one customer was there at any one time, it was hard lines for the rest of the sales team. There was a Second Sales and also a Third Sales, then came a Junior Sales, who unfortunately did not often get to show her selling skills unless the shop was very busy. Her job was also to keep the showroom in pristine condition and check that anything that was sold was replaced on the rails from the stockroom. For the junior, it was more a case of learning the trade, a kind of 'watch and learn'. As the sales ladies were dependent on the commission from sales, it was quite frustrating if customers drifted in one at a time. But it was such a lovely working environment that everybody seemed to enjoy their work.

Most of my co-workers were Jewish, and they were lovely

Diamonds in the Coal Dust

ladies. The older ones were married and most of their husbands were professionals, such as solicitors or dentists, but none of them were stuck up and there was no snobbery. I loved Mondays, as in the staffroom at lunchtime the young single girls would regale the rest of us with their weekend activities. I loved hearing about Lyons' Corner House. I didn't know where it was, but it sounded very glamorous and exciting. They would also go dancing at the Astoria. They were such pretty girls, and you could feel the energy bouncing off them as they chattered away. Sometimes one of the older ones would invite me and my friend, who was the Junior Sales, to her house after work. It all seemed very exciting.

In the days before decimalisation, nearly all our items ended in 19/6 or 19/11, and as there were no calculators at that time it was no easy task totalling up the sales columns at the end of the day. Nowadays, I find myself totting up lines of figures sometimes at night when I can't sleep. Today, if you go to the supermarket, the till even tells the assistant how much change to give – how times move on.

At the end of my working day, trouble would come if the cash in the drawer did not tally exactly with the account book. I was always on a tight schedule to catch my train – it was an hour's wait for the next one if I missed my regular one. Once particular night, my book didn't balance – it was two pence out. I checked and double-checked, but there it was. I must have given someone the wrong change. The manageress was calm and very patient while I became more and more upset. Eventually, she said that she would put the two pence in. I couldn't thank her enough and it made me extra careful to make sure it never happened again. I put the money in the leather wallet, and locked it and ran all the way to the bank, where I deposited the bag of money in the night safe before running all the way to the train station, where my travelling companions were waiting for me as usual with the train door open. The next day I apologised to my boss for my mistake, but a valuable lesson had been learned.

At the weekend, three or four of the girls from my village would go to the nearest cinema, which was twenty minutes away by train. On Saturday nights, we would go by train, but on Sundays the trains didn't run from our village, so we had to catch a bus. This entailed a thirty-minute bus ride to the stop nearest to the cinema, and then a thirty-minute walk to the cinema. The bus would pick up at a couple of villages before ours, and when we got on there would already be a few lads on the upstairs deck. They were loud, but one was louder than the others and he seemed to target me with his loud conversation. I wasn't really interested, as he wasn't my cup of tea. Not that I knew what my cup of tea was! But, as the months went by, he became friendlier and, for all his bravado, he seemed a little lacking in confidence.

My friend Jean, the Junior Sales at work, began inviting me to her home sometimes at weekends. She lived in the town, which I thought was very lively. Her parents were lovely people and she had a younger brother. We would go to the shops, and sometimes to the theatre. She seemed to have loads of freedom, I suppose because she lived in an urban environment. The trouble was that Jean wanted me to go home with her nearly every weekend and, apart from the fact that my aunt was not too keen on the idea, I sometimes wanted to do something different myself.

Eventually, the group of us who went to the pictures seemed to have paired up and it was taken for granted that Bill (the loud one from the bus) and I would sit together at the pictures; it was all still very casual though.

Things progressed quite slowly, but one day Bill said he would be coming to town and asked if he could meet me out of work. I told the girls in the showroom, and of course they were very interested and kept watching out of the window for him, giving me a running commentary as they watched. 'Oh, he looks nice' and 'He looks very nervous' were some of the comments relayed back to me at my desk.

The shop closed, and I cashed up and did my books. Fortunately, they balanced and I was ready for the off. 'Good luck!' all my workmates shouted. I felt strangely underwhelmed.

Bill came with me as I dropped the bank bags off at the safe. He asked me what I would like to do. I didn't know what to say, so I left it up to him. We went for a coffee and then went to the pictures. There were so many picture houses in town at that time that really we were spoilt for choice. There was the Scala, the

Diamonds in the Coal Dust

Odeon, the Ritz, and the Assembly Rooms (which was a little seedy, as it had a bit of a reputation for men going there on their own). There were also several theatres, including the Empire, the Theatre Royal, the Grand and the Varieties. We chose an easy-to-watch film and came out of the cinema in darkness. Outside the bus station was a man with a barrow who was roasting chestnuts. We bought a bag, conical-shaped with perhaps half a dozen chestnuts in; they smelled delicious. I thought later that the chestnuts were the best part of the evening.

The fashion house where I worked was on a very busy corner in the middle of the town, and, looking out of the windows, one would see crowds of people milling about. From the upper windows, they looked like ants, one line going one way and one the other. It seemed that our shop was a cocoon of calm, insulating everyone inside from the outside melee. It seemed like a separate world, especially to a seventeen-year-old.

Our manageress was like a mother hen. If anyone had a problem, she wanted to know about it, and if there was anything she could do, she would do it. But the rest of the ladies were also always available if any of the younger ones wanted a bit of advice or just wanted someone to listen. On the downstairs floor, undergarments were sold and it was all very discreet, with personal fitting rooms in case a customer needed the services of our qualified corsetière.

On the first floor, there was a small section which sold hats. Some of them were very grand. Sometimes ladies didn't want anything in particular, but just came for a chat or a cup of coffee. Many of them were regular customers, known by name and just dropping in to check new stock.

We had a small staffroom, and usually for lunch the Junior would be sent out with an order for sandwiches. Further down our street was Betty's café, and if anyone had a birthday it was the custom for that person to go to Betty's and buy cream cakes for their close friends. It seemed very exciting at the time.

Next door to the store was a Field's coffee house, where they used to grind different types of coffee beans to make all sorts of cups of coffee. The smell would drift into our store and it was heavenly; I can smell it now. So, going out of the store in my lunch hour gave me an insight to a world of different experiences. It doesn't seem all that fabulous, thinking about it all now. My buying ability was firmly kept in check by my meagre funds. I was paid £2/9/6p a week and nearly 10/- of that went on train fares. After my aunt got my board, there was not much left over. But it was good just to window-shop.

There was much excitement on the shop floor one Monday morning. Helen, the Third Sales, had become engaged to her boyfriend over the weekend. Everyone was anxious to see the ring. It was magnificent – a huge diamond – it was almost the most beautiful thing I had ever seen. The most beautiful thing for me was Helen. She had glossy, thick, dark hair, big dark-brown eyes and a lovely smiley mouth. She was so happy and everyone was happy for her.

One week, Jean had asked me to go to her parents' house for the weekend, but I had arranged to meet Bill. I don't think she was too impressed with my relationship with Bill. It was a Saturday night and, as usual, we went to see a film, had a coffee and then caught the bus home. As Bill lived in the next village, I got off the bus first and he stayed on to his destination. I got off the bus, oblivious to the storm that was awaiting me.

My aunt was waiting for me, and I knew something was brewing by the look on her face. She went straight into the attack. 'Where have you been and who have you been with?' she yelled at me. She knew I had been seeing Bill, so I didn't know what the drama was. It turned out that Jean and her parents were expecting me and when I didn't turn up they had contacted the police. Oh dear. It wasn't so much the fact that I hadn't been to Jean's, but the fact that the police had been to the house, which to my aunt was a scandal in itself. The drama did blow over, but I was annoyed with Jean for insisting that I was going to her house, even though I had told her I wasn't. I never stayed at her parents' house again, although I did apologise to them, and Jean and I always stayed friends. In fact, we are still in touch with each other to this day. Things became easier when she found a boyfriend herself.

Diamonds in the Coal Dust

Bill worked at the coal mine in our village – in fact, the same one that my uncle had worked at. When he left school, he had begun an apprenticeship as a fitter at a local brewery. He always wore a cap wherever he went. When he met up with me, the cap would be glued firmly to his head. He wouldn't have looked right without it. On his second week at the brewery, he got involved in a fight with one of the older men at the brewery. Apparently, the older man said something derogatory to Bill. He ignored the remark and the man came back with, 'If you can't fight, get a big hat.' That was like a red rag to a bull, so Bill punched him. He was immediately sacked and that was the end of his apprenticeship. As Bill's father said he had to get another job, he went to the pit.

He had to walk past my aunt's house to go to work and on his way home after his shift. As he finished work at 8.30 p.m., he would call in at our house and have a cup of tea or coffee and then I would walk with him to the bus stop. There was usually a collection of young men standing at the rec gates opposite the bus stop; it was a meeting place for teenagers. One particular night, I had seen Bill onto the bus and was walking home when I became aware of someone behind me. I began to walk faster, but this young man grabbed hold of my arm and swung me round. I was surprised when I saw who it was – a lad a few years older than me and very quiet, or so I had thought. There was nothing quiet about my reaction; my heart was pounding and I was screaming for all I was worth, my arms flailing about everywhere. He must have thought it wasn't worth the trouble, as he gave up and walked away. I dared not say anything to anyone, as I thought it would have been too much of a scandal. I did see the chap shortly afterwards and was pleased to see that he had a black eye, but no mention was ever made of it. I didn't walk Bill to the bus any more after that.

Now and again, a group of us younger ones would have a night out, especially if there was a particular heart-throb appearing at one of the theatres. One of the juniors excitedly told us that Slim Whitman was appearing at the Empire the following week. Wow! Slim Whitman, with the long black coat, the white silk tie and hair and moustache so black you could almost see the shoe

Maddy Worth

polish sitting on them. He was a big star, yodelling through 'Oh Rosemarie, I love you'. Three or four of us said we would go along, and we had a wonderful night. After the show, we queued at the stage door for his autograph. He didn't look so good close up.

The next morning at work, one of the girls told us that he had asked her to meet him. What! It was unbelievable that our little Helen had a date with Slim Whitman. Anyhow, our manageress got wind of it and called Helen to her office. 'Explain yourself, young lady. What are you thinking of, going to meet a man old enough to be your father?' Helen was very embarrassed, but didn't want to miss the opportunity, so our boss suggested to Helen that she should ask if someone could go along with her as a chaperone. Unsurprisingly, there was no answer forthcoming from the Slim Whitman camp. I believe a little later several stories emerged that were not very good news for the young Helen. It seems Mr Whitman had a bit of a reputation with young girls. We did go to other shows, but none of us was tempted to chance our arm with ageing 'stars'.

That summer, when I was seventeen and a half, Jean asked me if I would like to go on holiday with her and her family to Blackpool. I didn't see why not, but I did say I would have to ask my aunt if it would be OK. Bill was not too pleased about it. He asked me – no, pleaded with me – not to go. I, of course, said I was going and that was that. Jean and I were really looking forward to the holiday, but as it drew nearer Bill became more and more nervy. 'Can we get engaged before you go?' he asked. I was only seventeen and a half and did not think that my aunt would approve. However, he turned up one evening after work with a little box and showed me the ring inside. 'Will you wear this all the time?' he asked me. I didn't know what to say. I put it on my finger and turned it round. It was a pretty little ring, but I didn't feel any different.

When I showed it to my aunt, she didn't seem too impressed either and didn't say too much, except, 'I hope you're not thinking of getting married.' My colleagues at work were more excited than me, and oohed and aahed over me, saying that the ring was beautiful, which I thought was very sweet of them. They

Diamonds in the Coal Dust

were such lovely girls and they actually were sincere in their compliments. I didn't mind that they had rings with stones in them half the size of England.

So off we went to Blackpool, full of high spirits and great expectations. The first night at our hotel, we met up with a group of lads the same age as us. Jean's mum and dad seemed to like them and they were very polite. They had obtained tickets in advance for several shows, so it was arranged that one night Jean and one of the chaps would go to a show. The next night I would go with another of the lads. It was such fun and so light-hearted that the week flew by. I can't remember if the weather was good, but in those days it did not seem so important. Anyhow, at the end of the week I knew that I couldn't be engaged to Bill. It wasn't that I had met somebody else – in fact, we never heard any more from any of the Blackpool boys – it was just that I realised that there was so much going on out there. So, painfully, I had to come home and give Bill his ring back. Most people said that it was the right thing to do, as we were not really suited, and I think my aunt was not too unhappy about it, although she didn't say as much.

I didn't drift back into going to Jean's at the weekends, although we did have trips out with other girls at work. There was plenty to do; my circle of friends had widened and I was just enjoying myself, having a good time.

Four or five months later, I was Christmas shopping in my lunch hour and, among the throng of shoppers, who should I bump into but Bill. It was nice to see him and we exchanged pleasantries, just chit-chat really. He invited me to go for a coffee, but as my time was limited I declined. However, he did ask if he could meet me after work. Of course, when I arrived back at work and told the girls, they were agog and full of advice for me. Thirty minutes before the shop closed, they were looking out of the windows and relaying information back to me: 'He's not here yet' or 'We can't see him'. However, fifteen minutes before closing time, there he was.

I must admit that it was quite nice to pick up where we had left off. I did play it cool at first, but after a few weeks we settled into a familiar routine. Saturday night, he would meet me out of work and we would probably go to the cinema, and Sunday evenings he would meet me out of church and if the weather was OK we would walk up towards the moor, which was a picnic and meeting place for young ones.

A couple of times during the week, Bill would call at my house on his way home from work and stay for a couple of hours until it was time for his bus. Eventually, he asked me if I would wear his ring again, and it was accepted that we were now an engaged couple.

During the following summer, we began to think about getting married. In the meantime, my manageress left her position at the shop to take over another fashion shop in the city. I was very upset, as I felt as though I was losing a good friend. The new manageress was very nice, but things were not as comfortable as before. Shortly afterwards, my friend Jean told me she was leaving to join our old boss at her new store. I was asked not to mention it at work, as it could have been perceived that Jean had been poached by our friend, which I suppose she was really. I must admit I was quite unsettled at work by the changes and, after a visit to see Jean, my old boss offered me a position at the new shop as cashier/bookkeeper. I did feel a little deceitful as I made up an excuse for leaving, but I was very happy to join my friends at the new shop. It was a smaller place, but had a nice atmosphere.

As plans for our wedding went ahead, it was decided that it would be a small affair as money was quite tight. I was planning to wear a suit and have one of my friends as bridesmaid, also in a suit. However, Bill had a younger sister and he told me that she was upset that she wasn't a bridesmaid with a floaty dress. After some debate, it was suggested that one of the girls at work would lend me her wedding dress and also a bridesmaid dress for my friend. The manageress even had the dresses adjusted in the alteration room so that they fitted exactly. So my future little sister-in-law got to wear her floaty dress, the only one who had a new dress.

It was quite a nice day in September, and everything went pretty much according to plan. My grandma and grandpa on my father's side managed to come, even though Grandma was not very well. Afterwards, we left to go on the train to Blackpool for the week.

Diamonds in the Coal Dust

We were to live with my aunt initially, but Bill asked at work about the possibility of us getting a pit house, as most of the houses in our village were owned by the National Coal Board (NCB).

I returned to work after our week's break. Nothing seemed much different, but it was. Not many weeks later, I began to feel nauseous, especially in the mornings. I had become pregnant almost immediately and did I know it! Mornings were terrible, as were afternoons – in fact, most of the day!

Travelling on the train to work, I would be found hanging out of the window being sick – not very nice for me or my co-passengers either. The manageress was very sympathetic and allowed me to go into work a little later, but that didn't seem to help. People suggested to me that it would pass. In fact, the doctor said the same. He gave me anti-sickness tablets, but there was no marked improvement. He even tried sea-sickness tablets, but with the same result, no improvement. I soldiered on at work for four months, but eventually I had to call it a day. It wasn't fair to my workmates or to the manageress, who had bent over backwards to try to work around my condition. After about six months of pregnancy, it did get easier and I began to feel quite well, but I didn't seem to put much weight on.

A couple of months before the baby was due to be born, we were offered our first house to rent. It was quite a large house: three bedrooms, two large attics and a nice front room and living kitchen. In the kitchen sat a huge black-leaded cooking range. There was no hot water, no bathroom or indoor toilet, but it was bliss. The house had been occupied by two elderly gentlemen, one of whom had died there, actually in the outside toilet, apparently. It was obvious that nothing had been done to the place for donkey's years, but that didn't bother us.

We didn't have much money, but decided to decorate the two downstairs rooms and one bedroom for starters. Bill put wallpaper on the walls and did a good job of it. We had linoleum on the floor and, with our little bit of money, we bought a sideboard, table and chairs for the front room and a little three-piece suite. We thought it looked beautiful.

For the kitchen, someone gave us a little wooden table and

two huge horsehair armchairs which scratched the backs of your legs every time you sat on them. I bought some red-and-white checked gingham and made curtains, a tablecloth and a little curtain to fit round the stone sink, which was quite ugly. We just about managed to get shipshape before the baby arrived.

The annual fair in our village was always held on the weekend nearest to the end of June. Everybody turned out to wander round the stalls and amusements and try all the different fairground rides. The baby was due the weekend after the fair, so when Bill came home from work on the Friday evening, we decided to have a leisurely walk to the recreation ground where the fair was based.

It was nice to meander slowly round with the music blaring out everywhere we went. I suppose we headed home around 10 p.m. I felt that I wanted to go home, but I wasn't sure why, so I didn't say anything to Bill. At just after midnight, I was fairly confident that the baby was on the way and Bill hotfooted it to my aunt's house, asking her to come as soon as possible. I knew she would know what to do.

He then went to fetch the midwife, who lived a ten-minute walk away, but two minutes in her little Morris 1000. Bill didn't wait for her, but came dashing back on his own. I think he thought the baby would be there when he got home.

After around half an hour, the midwife arrived, complete with her bag of tricks and a bottle of gas for the gas and air, which was the only pain relief in those days.

After she had examined me, she assured us all that there was a long way to go and perhaps it would be better if we all got some sleep, including herself. I did sleep – fitfully, as I kept waking up to ask how much longer it would be. My aunt kept busy making cups of tea and the time seemed to go quite quickly.

I woke up at 7 a.m. and Bill was fast asleep. The midwife said that the baby would be born by 7.30 a.m. He was actually born at 7.20 a.m. and Bill was still fast asleep. Our little boy was so beautiful, only small, at 6lbs 4oz, but absolutely perfect. I did wonder whether my mother had been as thrilled when I was born; I would never know.

Bill woke up and was a bit miffed that he had missed it all.

Diamonds in the Coal Dust

Within an hour, I was enjoying a cup of tea and trying to finish the sweater I was knitting for Bill. I couldn't believe that an hour before there had been two of us and now there were three. How wondrous was that? About 9.30 a.m., the neighbours began visiting, eager to see the new arrival.

My aunt spent a part of each day with us, seeing that we had everything necessary for the baby. Bill decided to make a start on decorating the baby's room, which was quite small and at that time just had the baby's cot standing in it. It was decided that the baby should sleep in our room at first, until the room was finished and aired out. Some months before, we had ordered a pram and put a deposit on it. One was not expected to bring the pram into the house until the baby was born, as it was supposed to be bad luck. So Bill went on the train to bring the pram back from town. He travelled with it in the guard's van so that it would be safe. He was so proud when he came pushing the pram. It was beautiful, white, bouncy and shiny.

We called our son Martin and we loved him to bits; he was such a good baby. I would feed him and change him, and he would sleep through to the next feed. He was out in all weather except fog, in cold rain, even snow; he would be snuggled up in his pram with a little hot-water bottle.

When he was a month old, we went back to Blackpool for a holiday. It seemed strange that, less than a year before, we had been there on our honeymoon, and now we were three.

Back home I would get up very early and have the nappies washed and on the washing line before some people were even up. Two long washing lines would be stretched across the back yard of the row of terraced houses, stretching from the house to the outbuildings where the toilets were. The road was unmade, so that in winter it would be rock hard when it was freezing, but when it thawed it would be a quagmire. Quite often the coal wagon would come with a delivery of coal and instead of going round the back of the outbuildings the driver would plough through the washing line. Nappies and smalls would end up either adorning the bags of coal or laid in the mud. That was a very upsetting sight, as in those days to get your whites white you had to boil them in the copper with a bit of dolly blue, and that was after you had given the washing a going-over in the peggy tub with a posser. But nevertheless I loved Martin's baby days, and we would walk miles, pushing him in his pram, for I was always keen to make sure that he had as much fresh air as was possible. He never crawled as a baby; he would sit on his bum and then proceed to pull himself up. He was a stocky little chap and at thirteen months of age he set off walking on his own, into the big wide world. From then on there was no stopping him; he was a very adventurous child and would go missing if you took your eyes off him for a moment.

When Martin was eighteen months old, we had the chance to exchange our house for one on the front. It was actually the house of David and 'Twelve Street Rag' Liz (so-named for the record she had played over and over again when she arrived in the village). They had two little girls and wanted a bigger place. Their house had a nice private front garden which we thought would be good for Martin to play in. It did seem a good idea on the face of it. However, while Liz always had nice furniture and all the latest fashion in decor, underneath it all lurked a load of problems. The house itself was very damp, and when we took the linoleum up from the floor, we found several layers of old newspapers underneath, all quite wet – it smelled terrible. On the walls were several layers of old wallpaper which we had to strip right back before starting again.

At about the same time as we moved house, I discovered I was pregnant again. This time I didn't suffer from morning sickness. Again I didn't put much weight on, but that wasn't surprising with a very active toddler to chase after. When I was five months pregnant, the doctor thought that things were not progressing as they should, so I was sent to the maternity clinic. This journey involved two bus trips and a long walk, so it was not surprising that when I arrived at the clinic, juggling Martin and the pushchair, my blood pressure was sky high. However, they said everything was fine with the baby; I just had to take things steady – fat chance. I had arranged to have this baby at home as I did with Martin; I figured that as it had been plain sailing with his arrival, this second one should not be any different.

Diamonds in the Coal Dust

Two weeks before the baby was due, I felt the usual pains on a Sunday evening, nothing too severe, but Bill brought the bed downstairs in preparation. We didn't alert the midwife at this stage and, as the evening wore on, Martin was put to bed upstairs. He was in his own bed by now, which made the cot available for the baby. That night, the wind became very strong and everything in the house rattled. My labour progressed very slowly. At around 1 a.m. there was a terrific crash and Bill and I jumped out of bed to find that one of the bedroom windows had blown out. Martin slept through it. Bill wedged a piece of cardboard in the gap and we went back to bed. All day Monday I was really uncomfortable; the midwife came and checked me out and said that I was only in the early stages of labour. Monday went and I was feeling quite tired, as I hadn't managed to get any sleep and had spent most of Monday night prowling around. The next morning, Bill took Martin to my aunt's house and the midwife called again. She said that things weren't moving as fast as they should be. I really didn't need her to tell me that, but I was so tired that I could hardly think straight. However, with a little help from the midwife our daughter arrived, chubby and screaming and weighing 6lbs.

As I remember, she didn't stop screaming for months. I tried feeding, changing, and putting her in her pram, but she was having none of that. One sunny day, she was out in the pram in the garden. Martin was doing a spot of gardening with his bucket and spade; Nicola, our baby daughter, was not happy. In fact, she was only happy when she was being held, and I became very clever at doing everything with one hand, while she was tucked under my arm. She was a beautiful little girl with blonde curls all over her head and chubby rosy cheeks. But she didn't believe in sleeping, and if Nicola didn't sleep, nobody slept – except her dad, who could sleep through almost anything. As she grew and became heavier it became quite a struggle carrying her around all the time. Martin was an amiable little boy and was quite happy to occupy himself with anything in his toy box. He had a little tricycle and covered some ground on it with his little legs.

Time seemed to fly by, and the children grew into very different little characters, Martin very laid-back and Nicola making sure that everyone was aware of her presence. My aunt used to call her 'bossy-boots'. Bill was friendly with another miner who was interested in photography – he was always one for big boy toys was Bill – so he decided to take up photography as a hobby. He got all the bits and bobs; camera, enlarger, developer, the lot. It cost a fortune, but I must say that when the children were small, he did produce some lovely photographs. Eventually, though, he got fed up with it and went on to something else.

Nicola did not improve on her sleeping habits as she moved into her toddler years, and she began to have terrible night terrors. The children would go to bed without any trouble at all, but inevitably Nicola would wake up screaming and yelling that there were snakes in her bed – it was always snakes. We would cuddle on the settee, but if I closed my eyes she would wake me up, warning me that the snakes were coming. I was exhausted and a trip to the doctor's didn't help much, as he said that all children had nightmares. Well, Martin certainly didn't, and asking around my friends didn't help me in any way either.

We moved house again, this time next door to the one we exchanged with Liz and her family; thankfully she had got rid of her 'Twelve Street Rag' record. It was a nice big house with much more room for the children. I began helping out at the village shop a couple of days a week. Bill joined the fire brigade – as a part-timer, that is – if he wasn't at work, he was on call if the fire buzzer went off in the village, and he would run down to the station to man the fire engine. If there was a call-out during the night, the siren would not go off in the village; each fireman had an alarm fitted in their house. If it went off in the night, Bill would leap out of bed into his trousers and shirt and dash out of the house, usually leaving the door wide open. I suppose it was quite a sight – men running from all directions of the village in various states of undress towards the fire station – but time was of the essence. The first half dozen men to arrive got the fire engine revved up, opened the big double doors, jumped into their protective gear and were off to the emergency, all in a matter of minutes. Anybody arriving after the engine departed closed the doors and made sure everything was shipshape. They would sign on for a lesser fee than the men who had actually gone on the emergency, but Bill took it all very seriously – if he didn't get

Diamonds in the Coal Dust

down in time to ride the machine, he didn't want to know. We even had an agreement with our neighbour that, if the siren went off while I was at the shop, Bill would run off to the fire station and Liz would come in and stay with the kids. On hearing the fire buzzer while I was at the shop, I had to dash home to the kids. Bill had a full dress uniform which he wore if they turned out at weekends to service the water hydrants. He had a black jacket with silver buttons, black trousers and shoes – highly polished – and a peaked cap with a fire service badge on the front. Jacket and trousers were hung in the wardrobe after use and his cap left upside down on top of the television – until, that is, one day he found that our cat had been and done the thing that cats do in his upturned cap. He was mortified, but the kids and I had a laugh (on the quiet, of course).

When Martin was six and Nicola was four, I became pregnant again. On one of my regular visits to the antenatal class, it was found that my blood count was very low and it was suggested that it would be better for me to have this baby in the hospital. I had to have two injections a week up until the birth, in order to keep my blood count up. It was also suggested that there should be no more babies, as this one was going to be even smaller than the first two. I worked at the shop up to six weeks before the birth, and it wasn't very obvious that I was pregnant as I didn't put much weight on. I was extremely tired for most of the nine months and felt as though I was dragging myself around. Bill was not much of a house husband; his big love was fishing, he had also taken up bowls at the local green and he did like a drink after work. Liz, my next-door neighbour, had three girls by this time, slightly older than my children, and we would often take all the kids out walking. We would go for miles up through the woods where the children could run freely, picking bluebells and blackberries and hazelnuts. There was a shop which had opened in the old part of the village which was always called 'the new shop'. Off Liz and I would go with all the kids in tow, up to the new shop where we could purchase a ball of wool and have the rest of the amount needed 'put by' until we could afford it. The kids would probably get a bottle of pop or crisps, one or the other, as money always seemed to be sparse. Pop bottles were returnable at that time, so if the kids wanted anything and there was no money available, they would have to take a bottle back to the shop for 3d.

An elderly man came about twice a year around the streets with a horse pulling a roundabout on a trailer, and the children were encouraged by the man to take out a bundle of old clothes in exchange for a ride. It was a very serious business, and all the children would run home almost ripping the clothes off their mums' backs to pay for a ride. People didn't have wardrobes full of clothes in those days. The roundabout man was quite strict and if a child turned up with a couple of garments he would bellow, 'Not enough there, go get some more!' The terraced street we lived in had many children, as the houses were classed as family houses. Most of the families were decent, but some were not so decent, and their offspring would terrorise the more timid little ones in the street. It was not unusual for Martin to go out with a ball or a new toy and, in five minutes flat, it would disappear, never to be seen again. There would be physical misbehaviours as well, above and beyond the normal childhood spats. This was one of the reasons that Liz and I used to take the kids out of the way so often. But sometimes you just had to leave them to it and try to watch from a safe distance. One particular family had quite a few children ranging in age from about three years of age to the late teens. The youngest one, who was very tiny for his three years, was unbelievable; I think he walked on his own from the age of eight months, possibly because he was fed up of being trodden on and thought it was safer if he was up on two legs. He had a sister probably four years older than him, and they would be out in the street running riot. One day there was a commotion outside and when I went to investigate, two bigger lads had this three-year-old with a rope around his waist, and had thrown the other end of the rope over the wall of the outbuilding and proceeded to hoist this little lad up in the air. Everybody was laughing, even his own family, but I was horrified. How that child survived to adulthood I will never know, but survive he did. His elder sister was a nasty piece of work, and I believe she was expelled from school in later years. But really they didn't stand a chance, as there was never any adult supervision available. The older siblings were 'responsible', if that is the right word, for the younger ones.

Diamonds in the Coal Dust

At Whitsun, I would get new outfits for my two children: a suit and shirt for Martin and a dress and white shoes and little straw hat for Nicola. We would visit their grandparents on the Sunday and usually have a lovely day out. A couple of weeks after Whitsuntide, Martin had been out playing and came back with mud all over his shoes and put them on the window ledge outside to dry. They disappeared and it took probably two months for them to reappear on the feet of one of the lads up the street. Nothing but nothing was safe unless it was nailed down.

Two weeks before my third baby was due, we had been faced with very high winds; we felt it in our house as we probably lived in the highest street in the village. On the Saturday morning the rain came down, torrential rain which was unusual for July. I went to visit a friend in the next street who had just returned home after the birth of her second baby. She had been at her mother's house for two weeks to have the baby. When I returned home, the fire buzzer went off; Bill of course was the first off the mark. I did lunch for the kids and they played inside as it was raining. At about 2.30 p.m., I began to feel not very well. Bill returned home at 3 p.m. and said that they had been pumping water out of flooded properties. He had a sandwich, and I was just explaining to him that I didn't feel too good when the fire buzzer went off again. Off went my not-too-concerned husband again, and almost immediately I knew that I was in labour. I had to be careful not to frighten the children and I sat down with them in front of the television to watch a programme they were fond of. After a time I thought I should do something positive, so I lifted the tin bath down from the pantry wall, filled it with warm water and had a bath. I then checked that my bag was packed. I was feeling very nauseous and beginning to get very uncomfortable. Just after 5 p.m., Bill returned and I yelled at him to go and ring for an ambulance. I suppose it took about twenty minutes for the ambulance to arrive, and I will never forget looking out of the ambulance and waving to my kids, who were standing on the front step with their dad. The ambulance man who sat in the back with me was very kind and held a bowl for me as I threw up for the whole journey to the hospital. I was moaning with pain in between being sick, and the ambulance man was trying to rub my back. I felt like telling him to bugger off. When I arrived at the hospital it was panic stations, as it was obvious that the birth was imminent. My second little girl was born at 7 p.m. – a tiny 5lbs, but very healthy. The sister decided that as it was visiting time I should be left in the delivery room, and Bill could visit me there – of course, he didn't come. He rang up at 10 p.m. and was told that his daughter had been born at 7 p.m. He had apparently been out with the fire engine again and hadn't expected things to happen so quickly.

I was in hospital for ten days, and it was a good idea as it happens, as I had a nice rest, and my aunt was looking after Martin and Nicola. I felt much better when I went home, although I was very thin. I went to my little job at the shop when the baby was six weeks old. Nicola started school in September, so on the days I helped out at the shop I sometimes took the baby with me. She was named Ann and she was a very well behaved baby. I would leave her outside the shop in her pram (it was safe in those days) and most people would talk to her as they passed.

Bill decided he was going to buy a car; he hadn't passed his test, but friends said they would sit by him while he learned. The children and I were excited when he arrived home with the new car. I thought it would be the start of a new life, going off for rides at the weekend. But it didn't quite work out like that; Bill needed someone qualified to sit beside him, so it was usually one of his fishing friends, and they would go fishing for the day.

Nicola was still having her nightmares. Martin and Ann would sleep through the night, no problem, but Nicola was very troubled by her dreams. One night she woke up, but for some reason I didn't hear her, and her father went to her. He wouldn't sit up with her, so he lit her a little Kelly lamp which was lit by paraffin with a little glass chimney on it. He left it on her window ledge, but for some reason she picked it up. I heard her scream and jumped out of bed to find that she had set off downstairs hugging the Kelly lamp, and the collar of her pyjamas had caught alight and burned her chest. Bill dashed the flames out, we wrapped her in a blanket and Bill dashed out to the car with her. There was nothing much I could do but sit and wait for him to come home with her. I was worried sick. I stayed up for the rest

Diamonds in the Coal Dust

of the night, and at about 6 a.m. Bill came home with a very subdued Nicola. I suppose I could say that we were lucky, as it could have been so much worse. There was a small burnt patch on the top of her shoulder and a small area on her chest. It wasn't very nice to look at, and they had given Nicola a sedative to help with the pain. They hadn't put a dressing on it and she couldn't wear clothes on her top half, so she couldn't go to school. The doctor came regularly to check it and she had to go back to the hospital every few days. We also had a dressing-down from someone at the hospital for leaving a child alone with a naked flame. That was very upsetting, given the plight of some of the children in our street, as we thought we were good parents. Eventually the burn healed to a stage where it wouldn't improve any more, and that was when the hospital doctor decided it was time for a skin graft. It didn't take the graft long to heal, so Nicola wasn't in hospital very long. She was very brave and never complained throughout it all. Strangely she never had another nightmare after all that, and she soon returned to school.

We didn't have an indoor toilet and bathroom in the house we lived in, and as the children were growing up we decided to apply for a council property in the village, although we didn't hold out much hope.

We were still close friends with Liz and Dave next door. They had a cooker in their property but, because there was no gas supply in our village, they had to have bottled gas to supply their cooker. I was still doing my cooking on the range; I found it wonderful for Yorkshire puddings and Christmas cakes. Liz had everything modern as soon as it appeared in the shops. She had the biggest Christmas tree and the biggest television. Dave was a very hard-working man and a good provider.

One day I was in our house and there was an almighty bang – the house shook. I was just going to investigate when the door was flung open and Dave stood there, his face black and his spectacles hanging from one ear. Apparently one of the gas bottles had been leaking and the gas had exploded – it blew the door off and the window out. As luck would have it, Liz and the girls were out. Dave was very lucky that it wasn't more serious. Every so often Dave would go on a bender – not very often; I think it was probably when they had a fall-out. But one Boxing Day evening, Bill and his father had gone for a drink, the children were in bed and my mother-in-law and I were in the house. Suddenly there was an almighty banging from next door. Dave must have been out by himself and come back a little worse for wear, so Liz had locked him out of the house. He was kicking the door, shouting and using words not found in the dictionary. After a few minutes, he came to our door and started banging it, but I didn't dare open the door although I felt guilty for leaving him out there. Shortly after that episode, Liz told us they were moving to a different village some miles away, where they had bought a smallholding. I think that Liz wanted to get Dave away from the environment he was in. We were sorry to see them go, but we promised to keep in touch with them.

The owner of the little shop where I worked retired and it was sold to somebody else. My job was no longer there, but I had the chance of some seasonal work in the fields, picking potatoes; it was hard work but I enjoyed it. The farmer would pick half a dozen of us in the village and take us to the fields. We would walk down to the fields in twos, picking up potatoes in a wire basket, and then emptying the baskets into a trailer which followed us down the rows. At the end of the first day I could hardly move, I was so stiff. But after a couple of days it became easier and they were such a good bunch of women; we managed to have fun even though it was back-breaking. When it had been raining it was very difficult, as mud stuck to our wellies and the bottoms of our baskets, making them very heavy to lift. We would have a drink at 10.30 a.m. from the flasks which we took, along with sandwiches, and that used to last us the whole day. We had an hour for lunch and, if we were in a field close to a farm, the farmer would take us back in his jeep so that we could eat in the barn. Otherwise we just crouched down by the hedge. We were usually cold and always mucky, but very glad of the flask of hot coffee. Potato picking did become easier as the weeks went on, but it was the good humour that actually made the job easier and more bearable. It was a different kind of humour to that which I had been used to, a bit on the smutty side really, but it was good to be able to have a belly laugh.

Diamonds in the Coal Dust

One day, towards the end of potato picking, it had been snowing heavily and it was bitterly cold; you couldn't tell if you were picking potatoes or stones. At lunchtime the farmer took us back to the barn, but I was so cold that I thought I would die. Bill's aunt lived quite near the farm, so I decided to go to her house to get warm. She took me in and gave me some hot soup and stoked the fire up. My hands and face were burning, but it was a lovely feeling. After forty-five minutes I had recovered and she sent me back to work with two cardigans and a warm tummy. I felt a different person and I was able to start work again with a renewed vigour. I never forgot what Aunt Alma did for me that day, and I don't think that I have ever been quite so cold since then. The work was hard and conditions were dire but it was good to get a wage at the end of the week.

I soon got into a full-time working routine. Sometimes I would take Ann with me and sometimes, if the weather was too bad, I would leave her at home and Bill would take her to my aunt's when he went to work at 11 a.m. Martin and Nicola would go to my aunt's house after school for an hour until I arrived home. The potato picking lasted for five weeks, but I was thrilled when the farmer offered me the chance to stay on to do more seasonal work; I loved it. Round about this time, we were offered a council house. I was so excited.

The house had a living kitchen, a nice front room, three bedrooms and, unbelievably, a bathroom. This was luxury – an indoor toilet and bathroom. I was so glad to leave the old house, no tears, no regrets, and the children were very happy. Our front room was used for 'better days than Sundays' as my aunt used to say. We lived in the living kitchen which was quite big enough for us all. We only used the front room for entertaining and for Christmas. I loved Christmas. Sometime in November the children would begin sticking strips of coloured paper together to make chains, and I would get their requests for Christmas presents, which after being purchased would be obsolete, as they changed their minds two weeks before Christmas. Then there was the trip to see Santa Claus – Lewis's was the place to go, but you had to be very patient, as the queue would sometimes stretch from the basement right up to the third or fourth floor. There would be hundreds of eager children, patiently waiting to see the big man, except mine – all the way up the winding stairs, they would be pleading with me, 'Don't let me sit on his knee.' They only wanted to give their letters to his little helpers and get the half-crown present at the end of the grotto. They would press their backs against the walls of the grotto and, when Santa was busy with a 'good' little child, they would quickly escape through the exit. They didn't even like the idea of Santa going into their bedrooms, so stockings had to be hung downstairs from the mantelpiece. There is no feeling as great as watching your children opening their stockings on Christmas morning – pure magic. One Christmas, when Ann was probably two years old, Martin and Nicola had opened all their stuff and as Ann was still in bed they opened hers as well. It was a good job she was too young to know! I loved it when the children were little, they were such good fun.

I loved them to bits, and I found it a bit sad that Bill didn't get as much pleasure out of them as I did. He didn't seem to want to spend time with Martin. When I asked Bill why he didn't take Martin fishing with him, he would say either, 'He doesn't want to come' or 'He won't sit still'. So we settled into a pattern of working all week and at weekends Bill would probably go bowling on Saturday mornings, call at the pub or the bookies or both, and then on Sundays he would usually go fishing. I would probably do the washing on Saturdays and housework on Sundays, ready for work again on Monday.

As Bill was a miner, we would get a load of coal once a month as part of his allowance. All of the houses in our street had a coal fire. Bill worked the afternoon shift and inevitably our load of coal would be delivered after he had left for work. I would come home from the fields to find a ton of coal piled up on the drive. As we shared a drive with the people next door, the coal would usually be blocking their drive as well, so I had to start throwing it into the cellar. If I wasn't tired when I got home from work, I certainly was by the time I had shovelled the coal in – I had muscles like Popeye.

If it was hard working in the fields in the winter, it was no less so in the heat of summer. One week, I was hoeing in the field – I

Diamonds in the Coal Dust

was on my own as there was only enough work for one. I had taken Ann with me – she was three years old at this time. She sat in the shade of the trees with her toys and her juice. The sun was extremely hot and, at the end of the day, one of my arms felt strange. While I was preparing tea my arm began to swell to almost twice its normal size. I went to the doctor, who told me that I had sunstroke on my arm as I had been in the same position all day with the sun repeatedly beating down on my arm. I was fine after a couple of days of treatment and rest.

The children went to Sunday school at church and Martin was in the choir. He actually sang solo at the carol service one year – I was so proud of him. The Sunday school would put on a pantomime in the village and Martin would usually have the male lead. Most of the other lads didn't seem to fancy performing. The girls would also take part, but I used to get annoyed as, every time the girls went to rehearsals, they would come home in raggy grey vests. When I used to get annoyed, Nicola would say, 'But they were the only ones left.' Obviously some kids were smarter than mine and came in 'holier than thou' undies, but went home in nearly new ones. Sunday nights would be hymn nights, as after they had been to Sunday school, usually when they were in the bath, we would be treated to the full repertoire.

Our neighbours were elderly, but very nice, and they had a daughter with Down's syndrome. She was a lovely girl who they had brought up to be quite independent.

We had a cat which we shared with our neighbours; he was a great character, but a free spirit. He had been missing for a couple of days and when he came home he was in a dreadful state, with one torn ear, a lump under his eye and fur missing everywhere. The vet said that he had been in a fight with another tomcat. He patched him up, gave him an antibiotic injection and put a big collar on him so that he couldn't lick his wounds. He advised us to have him castrated as soon as he was well enough. He shouldn't have said that in front of the cat, though, as the day before he was due to be 'done' he disappeared again, collar and all! This time he never came back. Martin had a rabbit which was kept in the back garden in a large hutch; it wasn't very friendly – well, not to me anyway. We also had a hamster at one stage; this was kept in a cage on the cupboard top. I was in the process of knitting an Arran jumper for Martin and I must have left it a little too close to the cage as, when I came in from work one day, the hamster had managed to get at it through the mesh of his cage, and had eaten a large piece out of the middle of the back. Shortly afterwards it escaped from its cage – perhaps it didn't like the colour of the wool.

Because we mainly lived in the kitchen, our front room was only usually used when we had visitors. I was expecting my in-laws for tea one day and had set the table and prepared salad, but when we came to sit down for tea, I discovered that Ann had taken a bite out of every slice of ham on each plate. Oh, the embarrassment! On another occasion, I had invited a friend to come home with me after work for tea. Nicola decided she wanted to help and started to prepare things but we had a laugh when she told me she could not find any tomatoes for the salad, so she'd opened a tin of tomatoes. Happy days!

When Ann was four years old, I had the chance to work for Avon Cosmetics for the Christmas period. Initially I was employed from September to December, which was very handy for Christmas spending. I started work in the editing office, which was the office that the orders came into. My job was to check the orders and payment slips as they came in, to make sure they were correct. Many of the ladies in our village were employed there, and a bus would pick us up in the village, taking us right to the doors of the factory. My aunt agreed to have Ann, and the other two would go to her after school. I loved it; I hadn't realised how good it would feel to go to work in decent clothes and come home without soil under my fingernails. The girls in the office were very friendly and it was a lovely environment. My aunt would meet me off the bus at home time with the kids and we would all go up to my house, with my aunt invariably staying until bedtime after having dinner with us. She didn't have a television set, so really there was nothing much for her to go home for. Bill would arrive home from work at 8.30 p.m. Sometimes the kids would be in bed and I know he resented my aunt being there every night, but she looked after Ann while I was

Diamonds in the Coal Dust

at work. How could I say to her that she wasn't welcome every night? However, after Christmas I was offered a permanent job at Avon, and Ann was due to start school after Easter, so everything was changing once again.

Bill still went fishing most Sundays and I would catch up with the housework. Sometimes I would take the girls to the cinema or shopping to Leeds. Martin became a devotee of Leeds United Football Club and liked to go to as many weekend matches as possible. We were lucky that a local couple, who had no children, took Martin under their wing and kept an eye on him, especially when he went to the away matches. He saved every ticket and programme, and they adorned his bedroom walls along with his Rod Stewart pictures. Martin was not much trouble, but if he did get a telling off and was sent to his room, he would strip his walls of all his posters and Leeds programmes. When he got over his mood, he would put them all back up again.

Avon had a very good sports and social club, and they would have various functions throughout the year. Each member of staff would also get a day off for their birthday. It was a very good firm to work for. There were about twenty ladies in our office, sitting at individual desks. Some of the ladies would go to evening classes to learn dressmaking or soft furnishing or even cake icing.

In our lunch hour, some of us would get the benefit of the skills which the different ladies were learning. The office would be converted into a cutting room and demonstration area, where we would all be busy with our different interests. One lady showed us how to make velvet cushions with a ruched effect, some square, some round like a cartwheel. Sometimes the fluff from the soft toys we were making almost choked us. It was a shame that work interfered with our hobbies, but for the most part it was a lovely light-hearted atmosphere. We had a supervisor who sat with her desk facing us, keeping a beady eye on things. On Fridays, one of my friends and I would go the nearby pub at lunchtime; nothing too heavy – just a sandwich and a shandy. We always came out in decent time to be back before work started. The trouble was that there was a railway crossing between the pub and the office, and it was always our bad luck that the gates were usually shut for a train to pass. Even though we would run all the way back to the office, the other ladies would already have their heads down, working. We would peep through the office door, and the supervisor, sitting with her back to the door, would purse her lips and say, 'You're late, ladies,' as we crept past her into the office. We were so terrified – not!

When it was the annual gala day, my friend Barbara and I would enter anything and everything. My girls would be in the fancy dress competition, and Martin would be in the sports section. One year, Barbara's husband and Martin were entered into the pram race. It was over about four miles, and Barbara's husband had managed to acquire an old pram. All I can say about it is that it had four wheels – well, it did when they set off. Martin was dressed as the 'baby' and David set off at a smart pace pushing him. They were doing quite well, but about halfway round the course, Martin and David swapped over so that David was the baby. Unfortunately, he was tipped out of the pram when a wheel came off, so they limped home on three wheels. But it was great fun and they did get second prize. Barbara and I were entered in the three-legged race; Barbara had plenty up top and I wasn't too far behind. Her mother-in-law had a ciné camera (it was before the days of video cameras) and she waited at the finish line. We won the race, but when it was replayed on the ciné, it looked like four ferrets fighting in two sacks as we belted up the track.

Avon was an American firm and there was no union representation on the premises. While I loved my time at Avon, I believe that some workers were not happy, mostly on the production line. Word would go round that the taxi had been called, and the offending member of staff would not be seen again – no discussion, end of story. For myself, I couldn't imagine anyone not being happy there; it wasn't like work, and the pay was good. Friendships I made there have lasted me all of my life.

Bill and I kept in touch with Liz and Dave, and we still visited them occasionally. The kids loved to run free round the place, watching the little pigs and running round with the horse. Liz and I would walk down to the local pub with the men for an hour. I was never a drinker, and never knew what to ask for if we went out. I would say, 'I'll have the same as Liz.' She would drink something called a Pony – I don't know what was in it, but I

Diamonds in the Coal Dust

would have been happy to sit over one all night. But Liz would say, 'Drink up, come on.' I felt so ill after three of them, I don't remember going home, and I never had a Pony again. They didn't seem to affect Liz, though. The other three were all smokers as well, and my throat would be sore for days after a night out with them. I used to think that it wasn't fair that Bill drank like a fish, and I used to get headaches, and he smoked and I coughed. I admired Liz and Dave and the fact that they had managed to move away from the 'mining men only' ethos.

Bill and some of his workmates would annually go on a weekend trip to London, to watch the rugby final at Wembley. It was a typical boys' trip, and there were wild tales of what they got up to. One of the wives told me that the women had an annual trip that went to Blackpool, and suggested that I went with them on their next trip. I mentioned it to Bill and he didn't seem to mind. My aunt said that she would help out with the kids when the time came. I was really looking forward to it, as it wasn't very often that I was 'let loose' on my own. The trip was from Friday night to Sunday night, and we sang songs on the bus, all the way there and all the way back. I had lost my voice by the time I arrived back home, but I had a fabulous time. I did miss my kids, though, and spent most of the weekend looking for presents for them. Some of the ladies on the trip were really daring; I had never laughed so much in my life. We would all finish up in one room in the hotel, and I remember one younger female being helped into a sling, which I think was part of the fire escape, while a couple more of the women tried to lower her out of the window. It's a wonder we didn't get banned from the hotel – or perhaps we did, I can't remember. But it was a great chance for me to let my hair down, which I wasn't accustomed to doing.

When Martin was eleven he was invited to sit for the exam which would gain him entry into the grammar school which I had attended as a child. I think there were four children along with him who attended. A couple of months later, they were invited to an interview at the grammar school. I was very proud of him, but unfortunately it all came to nothing, as later that year the school ceased to be a grammar school and became a high school, which was a glorified comprehensive. It was very disappointing, and a huge new school was built to accommodate older pupils from surrounding villages, who were sent en masse regardless of their ability. Martin fitted in OK, but there was none of the pride and traditional regime or the character-building of a grammar school. He joined the school football team, still supported his beloved Leeds United, but never seemed to shine academically even though he was very intelligent. Nicola began having piano lessons and really enjoyed that, but she wasn't to be persuaded to keep up her practice.

The two older children became interested in the different fads and fashions of the day. Since I was working full-time, I could indulge them to a certain extent and if anything was 'in' it would mean a trip on a bus into town, and then a tramp around the shops as the desired object would always be elusive; either it would be just sold out or it was expected next week, This was in the days of Doc Marten boots, Harrington jackets and fish tail parkas. But I was always popular when we managed to track down the much-desired item. All this went completely over Bill's head. If I said to him that one of the kids needed a pair of shoes, he would say, 'What do you want me to do?' But I do remember once when he had a win on the horses, he bought Ann a new coat with a hood, without even being asked – I was so excited that I will never forget it. He was a good worker, but it was the mining ethos which ruled: 'Work hard, play hard!' There was also a very crude saying that Bill used, which loosely translated meant that if you kept your woman poorly dressed but happy in bed, they would not stray. One of the things I didn't like was the vulgarity of some of their conversations. But, and it's a big but, they were the salt of the earth.

Ann had been experiencing quite a lot of tummy problems, and I had visited the doctor several times with her. However, one Saturday night she woke up screaming and obviously in great distress. My aunt had come as she usually did for her tea and to watch TV. Bill was off doing what he did on Saturday nights. I went to the phone box and phoned for the doctor. He had just finished examining her when Bill arrived home, a bit worse for wear. He proceeded to give the doctor the benefit of his experience until the doctor turned around and said quite loudly, 'Sit down and shut up.' Bill did as he was told, and I began to apologise for him. The doctor said to me, 'Don't you apologise for him, I am used to dealing with men like him.' I was so embarrassed. Ann settled down after the doctor left; he seemed to think that it was something she had eaten. The following week, Ann seemed OK, so I began to think that the doctor was probably right. However, come Saturday night she again became very ill, and when the doctor came out again he suspected that it might be appendicitis, even though she was so young. An ambulance was called and she was taken to hospital, where the doctors were not convinced that it was her appendix. But they did agree that something was going on and that they could not risk doing nothing, so they took her appendix out. She got over the operation, but as she grew up her stomach trouble was to reappear with a vengeance.

When Martin was thirteen, Nicola started at the same school as him, and she soon settled in as she was a popular eleven-year-old. Ann had reached the grand old age of seven and was still at the little village junior school.

One or two families in the village, and also some of Bill's workmates, were talking about emigrating to Australia. By this time, Bill had been to technical college and qualified as a mining deputy, which enabled him to use explosives to blast the coal out from the seam. The pay wasn't a lot more, but the whole package was much better. However, the pit in our village was very old and the wages were only made worthwhile by the bonus which miners received depending on the production of coal. Bill's old mine was almost worked out, so there was not much in the way of a bonus to be had. So the talk of moving to Australia became more frequent. Bill decided to reply to an advert in the paper for miners in Australia and see how it went. I don't think at that stage any of us thought that anything would come of it. The girls were quite excited about it, but Martin was not; it might never happen. But I thought it would be the chance of a new and exciting life for us all. Another of Bill's work colleagues had replied to the same advert so we could compare notes as and when things developed.

It wasn't straightforward; there were many ifs and buts, and the other family had a slight advantage as they already had relatives living in Australia. Bill had two jobs in the running, one as an ordinary miner working in a place called Wollongong in New South Wales, the other as a mining deputy in the Hunter Valley, working at a place called Cessnock. We did our homework and checked every pro and con – or so we thought. The job in Wollongong meant we would have to live in a sort of holding camp until we obtained our own house. In Cessnock, Bill would go as a deputy and there would be a house with the job. Bill and I went to London for the job interview, and while we waited for the results of the interview, we had to go with the children to Australia House for a vetting procedure. We couldn't prepare for anything, as everything had to come together at the same time for us to be able to go. The mining company would sponsor our journey if Bill got the job, but then it was up to the Australian government to give the go-ahead. Martin was still not very keen on the idea, as he didn't want to be parted from his beloved Leeds United. Also he said that he would miss all his pals. I think it was very disruptive for the children at their age, especially the older two. We finally got word from London about the interview, and Bill was offered the job in Cessnock. There would be a company house, and also help in transporting any possessions that we wanted to take. We all had to have medicals and chest X-rays, and references had to be checked. We finally got the all-clear but had to wait for notification of the actual date. It was expected to be in around two months' time, which was not long when you take into account everything that had to be done. We had to decide which of the children's special things could go, as obviously we couldn't take everything. We also had to decide what furniture would be going with us. We had collected plenty of literature, including a book describing the city of Cessnock. It was the third largest city in New South Wales, and was said to have a very good high school and two junior schools. The climate was described as being highly humid, as Cessnock was located in a valley created millions of years ago by a volcano erupting. Advice given to would-be immigrants was to make sure that any packing case sent from the UK should be specially constructed of treated wood and

Diamonds in the Coal Dust

lined with tar paper to ensure that we would not be importing any creepy-crawlies. It had to be big enough to hold our personal stuff, including, of course, Bill's fishing rods, etc. We were also taking the automatic washing machine, as it was almost new, two beds and the dining room suite. When I told one of my friends at work about the kerfuffle with the packing case, she was most amused. One of her neighbours and his wife were due to go to Australia round about the same time as us. Chris, who was the man of the house, was, my friend said, constructing his own packing case from spare pieces of wood. He had even been back and forth to my friend's house, cadging six-inch nails. Of course, we said that the Australian authorities would not allow it into the country, but they were undaunted.

We were becoming quite anxious, as we still had not received a definite departure date. Bill and I had to give notice to work, the children's schools had to be informed, and we had to book a haulage firm to collect the stuff that was being shipped out. Most important of all, we had to dispose of anything that we weren't taking. Things came to a grinding halt when there was a national postal strike. Everything was put on hold, as no mail was coming through whatsoever; it was very unsettling. When my boss asked me how things were going, I had to explain to him that it wasn't very good. 'No problem,' he said. 'Go into my office and ring the head office of the immigration department in London.' I did as he suggested, and in ten minutes I had been informed of our departure date and also the flight numbers. It was all systems go.

My friend in the office suggested that we should meet up with her neighbours. They were going to join their married daughter and her family in Wollongong, which would be a few hundred miles from us, but not too far by Aussie standards. We arranged to have a night out with them before we went.

We were to stay with my aunt for three weeks before we went, as we reckoned that with the three weeks that we had and the two weeks we were to stay in a hotel in Australia, our things should not be far away at the end of it.

The night out that we had with Chris and Mona was a great experience. They were an elderly couple and real characters, not at all phased by the prospect of going to the other side of the

Maddy Worth

world. My friend had told me a little bit about them; they had a motorbike and sidecar and would set off on a Sunday, not even knowing where they were going, spend the day on the coast and then set off back home. She said that they would invariably break down, but it was no problem to them; they would either bed down in a hostel or some kind person would take them in for the night. The saga of the packing case did not seem far-fetched, after all. But you couldn't help but love them. As my aunt would say, 'God loves a trier.' We promised to keep in touch with them once we got to Australia; they were going a week before us.

My friends in the office arranged a night out as a farewell do for me, and we went to the Variety Club to see Max Bygraves. We had a lovely night, though it was a bit sad, and I had some photographs as a memento.

It was all a bit manic for the last week or so. We had a get-together with the in-laws and a last minute get-together with Liz and Dave. My aunt had a senior citizens' trip on the day we were leaving; she didn't want to go, as she wanted to see us off. I urged her to go on the trip, as we didn't want anyone to see us off – we thought it would be too upsetting, and, as it happened, it was the right decision – when we set off in the train to London, it was as though we were just going on a day trip. But of course we weren't!

On the train we were all very subdued, a little excited and very apprehensive. It was Martin's fourteenth birthday and he didn't want to be there. We were on the train for four hours and then had four hours to kill in London until we had to leave for the airport. We managed to see the changing of the guard at Buckingham Palace and had lunch and a quick look around, then it was off to Heathrow.

It was all new to us, as we had never flown before and we didn't really know what to expect. The airport was buzzing with people – masses of them. We found the flight and checking-in details and we all trooped through, checking in our huge cases. It suddenly began to feel very real. We had time for a coffee and a few nibbles before we were called to board our plane. It was huge and we gripped each others' hands nervously. We looked for our seat numbers; we were all placed together, three seats and two seats side by side with an aisle separating us. We were positioned towards the back of the plane. We were advised to make ourselves very comfy, as we had a long journey in front of us. It would be thirty-one hours before we arrived in our new country.

The children were very good, and enjoyed the meal which came on a tray. Considering that none of us had flown before, they didn't seem to be at all nervous. The girls slept for a good part of the journey. When I went down to the front of the plane to find a toilet, it was like a different world. They had obviously seated people with babies all together at the front – there were babies everywhere, and the smell of wet nappies was almost overpowering. I was glad we were sitting at the rear.

We stopped for refuelling in Saudi Arabia and we were allowed to get off the plane for an hour, just to go into the airport, where it was stifling. The next stop was in Darwin, Australia.

Chapter Three

There were kangaroos hopping around everywhere – yes, this was Australia. There were men walking around the airport with collars and ties but with shorts and three-quarter socks. It looked very strange to us, but apparently it was the summer dress code for businessmen. We had ice-cold cokes and a leg stretch before returning to the plane for the final leg of our journey. Bearing in mind that we had never flown before, we all tolerated the journey remarkably well, but I was absolutely whacked as I hadn't slept at all. Sitting in front of us on the plane was a lady with two young girls and before we were due to land they disappeared to the toilets; they came out some time later having changed their dresses and wearing little straw hats – they looked like models and had obviously done it all before. We got off the plane looking crumpled, grubby and not very cheerful.

We waited in the luggage collection hall, and that was a real eye-opener. While we had packed our belongings in sturdy, well-labelled suitcases, the array of possessions coming down the luggage belt was mind-boggling. There were cardboard boxes tied up with string that had come apart, and plastic bags that had burst. It reminded me of my friends and neighbours who had made a packing case out of pieces of wood.

The manager from the colliery was collecting us from the airport. He was an affable Aussie who kept saying 'G'day' to everybody. He packed us into his car and off we set at a rate of knots. He pointed out places of interest as we flew along the highway. We stopped after forty-five minutes and had a cool drink; the kids had milkshakes. The scenery was beautiful, but I seemed to be the only one who was feeling queasy. It didn't help that I was riding in the back of the car, which was never a good idea for me.

We finally approached Cessnock; it was quite a let-down after

Diamonds in the Coal Dust

digesting the details of the book which we had read back home. We had had a preconceived idea of how Cessnock would look, and this was not it. Mr Greenhalgh – Bill's manager – turned off the road and drove down a track. 'This is your house,' he said. It was a large, rambling, weather-beaten, detached place. It had a veranda running round all four sides and it was totally fenced off, with huge trees running along the fence – a bit spooky, really. The kids thought it was fabulous. We then moved off and came back to the main road. 'This,' he said, 'is Cessnock.'

'Not Greater Cessnock?' I asked.

'Yep.'

It was like something out of a wild west film, with one very wide street with an assortment of shops and bars down each side. When we pulled up outside the hotel, I half expected to see a horse tied up outside. The hotel was more like a cowboy saloon with swing doors going into it. We were introduced to the lady behind the bar and she offered to show us to our rooms. We had two adjoining rooms. All the beds were singles, just iron bedsteads. I felt like crying but I didn't. We had a quick wash and brush-up and then went down for our evening meal. A lady came to us and read the choices out. I don't remember much of it except that every dish had pumpkin in it. I couldn't eat anything, I felt sick and I couldn't keep my eyes open – I just wanted to go to bed and never to get up again. Jet leg had kicked in big-time, and it wasn't long before we went to bed. As I lay looking at the ceiling, I wondered what we had let ourselves in for.

Night turned into day. The girls were still asleep and I went next door to check on Martin, who had been outside exploring.

'What did you see?' I asked him.

'Not a lot,' he said.

Around lunchtime we managed to get motivated, and after lunch it was time to begin the rest of our lives. I still felt jaded but Bill had the keys to the house so we decided to try to find it. It was a forty-minute walk out of town. Fortunately it was June, which meant winter in Australia; it would not have been much fun in the heat of summer. It was nice and warm but not too hot to get about. I actually felt better out and about in the fresh air. Vincent Street was a long wide street which ran straight through

Cessnock, so it led to everywhere. We followed the main road round and out of the village, through Aberdare, past the high school which Martin would be attending – it looked very nice and well built. I was glad Bill knew where we were going, because I hadn't a clue. We followed the little lane down the side of the high school (I would come to know it very well) and on through a pit yard, eventually coming to our property.

It was huge. The grass around the whole of the property was long – Bill had been told that he must get it cut. The house was on the edge of the bush, and snakes and lizards and spiders loved the long grass. We stuck to the path and walked down to the front of the house, onto the veranda. Down the side of the house, the double doors led into the kitchen diner – obviously nobody had lived in the place for some time. The kitchen opened on to a lounge with a large fireplace, and an old moquette three-piece suite had been left in there. Through the hall, there was a bathroom on the left. It was quite a nice modern bathroom, with a vanity unit and bath and shower, but no toilet. Straight down the hall and to your right were two double bedrooms. On the left was the biggest room I had ever seen; it was like a ballroom. It had a fireplace at either end and a dark polished wood floor. Back up the hall and to your right, opposite the lounge, was another bedroom, where an iron bedstead had been left, and also a baby's cot. From this room, a door opened on to the back veranda and the toilet. There was also a laundry room. Martin claimed the single room as his, although I felt it a bit far away from the rest of the house. Outside were two garages, two paddocks and a tennis court. There was a fire hydrant in the middle of the back garden, and a fire break had been cut deep about five feet from the perimeter fence.

We decided we would gradually move our belongings from the hotel to the house, but we needed transport. Bill bought an old banger – an automatic – it was good to be mobile. He also bought a lawnmower and set about clearing the grass. Behind the tennis court, he came across a goanna, which is a large lizard a bit like a small crocodile. He picked it up on a stick and came to the house to show it to the kids. Ann started screaming and locked the kitchen door and wouldn't let anybody in. She didn't like any sort of creepy-crawly.

Diamonds in the Coal Dust

I made the most of the laundry room and washed our clothes out daily by hand – the washing machine was still on its way. There was a very large rotary drier in the backyard and by the time I had finished pegging the last lot of washing out, the first lot was almost dry.

We got to know the town, and the kids loved the Carousel Bar, which was near our hotel. They could buy a 'Pluto pup', which is sausage on a stick, and they were partial to the flavoured milk which was also a speciality of the bar.

After we had been in Australia for a week, Bill had to start work. I couldn't drive, but most days we would go to the house, where there was plenty of room for the children. We would be back at the hotel for the end of Bill's work day and we would all have the evening meal in the hotel together. One evening when Bill came home, he brought someone with him, an elderly man called George. He had begun working at the same pit as Bill a few weeks before him. He thought we might like to meet his family, who had moved to a house on the other side of Cessnock. They were English, too, or 'Poms' as the Aussies called us. They had lived in Australia for fifteen years. George came to work in the gold mines in Western Australia ten years before, and then they moved to South Australia to Whyalla. They had a grown-up daughter who was divorced and had a two-year-old little boy. George and Monica also had a son who was ten years old. Apparently Jan, the daughter, had had an acrimonious relationship with her ex-husband and he had been harassing the family, so they had decided to up sticks and move to New South Wales. We arranged to go to see them the next day.

George and Monica also lived in a company house, smaller than ours and raised up off the floor. They had brought most of their furniture with them from South Australia. Monica was a Geordie and life had not been easy for her, but she was very feisty. George was much quieter and more of a listener. It was nice to meet some Poms who had been in Australia for a while and knew the running a bit more than us. They didn't sound very English any more, and Ian, who had been born in Australia, spoke like a 'fair dinkem' Aussie. We left them telling them that we would be pleased to see them at our house once we moved in.

I arranged for Martin to attend the high school and the girls were both to go to the junior school, which didn't please Nicola as she had already done a year of high school in England. However, in Australia they start high school a year later. We had to do a quick shop to get them kitted out in uniforms and also had to provide books and stationery.

After two weeks, we had to leave the hotel and move into the house, even though we had none of the essentials – we were still waiting for some notification of when we could expect our stuff to arrive. Bill tried to make enquiries but didn't get very far – in fact, he got nowhere. Nobody seemed to know where our stuff was and we had no telephone to contact anybody. We felt that we were up the creek without a paddle. Bill asked the pit manager if he could find anything out, but it seemed that we were on our own and had to get on with it. For the first few nights in our new house, Nicola slept in the single bed that was left in the house. Ann slept in the baby's cot and Martin slept on the two armchairs pushed together. I slept on the settee and Bill slept on the floor. As it was winter, it was quite chilly at night even though it was quite warm by day. We found a mound of coal which had grass growing through it out in the yard, and managed to light a fire in the lounge at night when we all bedded down. We had no duvets or blankets, as they were all coming in the packing case, wherever that was. It was obvious that we had to make a more permanent arrangement, given that there was no guarantee that our possessions would turn up at all. Monica and George lent us a mattress, which Bill and I slept on – on the floor – and I visited the charity shop in town and bought two single beds, a kitchen table and chairs. I went to the local store and bought some cheap bedding, and all of a sudden we seemed to be living in luxury. But we didn't expect to rough it for long, as we half-expected our belongings to turn up any moment.

Once the children started school and Bill was at work, I had nothing to do. I wouldn't see a soul until the kids came home again. The weekends were lovely: we would go into town to do the shopping and probably call and see Monica and her family. Perhaps it does not seem very exciting, but for me just having them all home all day was wonderful.

Diamonds in the Coal Dust

The kids settled in well at school, and in no time at all Nicola was speaking with an Aussie accent. We were still trying to track down our elusive belongings but not having any luck. After Bill had been at work for about three weeks, the miners began industrial action and began a pattern of working one day and striking the next. This was something we hadn't bargain for – we thought we had left all that in England. However, after a couple of weeks it was resolved. Nicola and Ann had already made friends at school and Martin had got into the school football team. Bill had workmates who were keen fisherman, but on a much grander scale than he had been used to. Their idea of a fishing trip was to pack up their tackle, take a large keg of beer and go for a weekend.

Australia was very much a male-orientated country, and some pubs had rooms where women weren't allowed. Men didn't ask the little woman's permission to go off at any tangent they wanted. It was obvious that I was going to have to organise something for myself that would occupy my time and make some money. I would spend hours wandering the property, feeling totally isolated and very sorry for myself. Some days I would walk into town and then get a cab back home. There was a bus that the children used for school – the 'bunnies' bus' – but it didn't run regularly, so sometimes the kids would walk to school.

One of my lifelines, especially in the early days, was the mail. Our letters went to the pit office and Bill had to collect them from there. Each evening when he came home I would ask him, 'Is there any post?' I did receive many letters and I wrote lots. My aunt wrote on a regular basis, but she wasn't much of a letter writer. Her letters usually consisted of 'Hope you are keeping well, as I am, well, that's about it for now.' Hardly worth the stamp it cost her to send it – but there it was, on a regular basis, written in her own thoughtful, neat handwriting and very much appreciated. Me – I never know when to stop writing. I start off really neatly, and by the end of the missive it's illegible. Those letters from my faithful friends and family kept me going in the early days.

I started getting the local press from the newsagent's, and happened to see an advert for vineyard workers. I didn't know anything about vineyards, but reckoned that the work couldn't be much harder than working in the fields back home. I showed it to Bill when he came home, but he didn't think it was such a brilliant idea. Pokolbin, where the vineyards were located, was about eighteen miles from where we lived and I hadn't a clue as to how I would get there, but we decided to have a ride out there to find out a bit more about it. We had actually been out to the vineyards one Sunday. George told Bill that different vineyards had visitors, say on Sunday, when you could drive around them all sampling the different wines for free. There was no pressure to purchase if you didn't want to. George called it 'a free drink' – he didn't have much fun in life.

We found the vineyard which was advertising for workers; it wasn't up and running at that time, as it was a new venture. The manager said that he was looking for six women workers. Part of the vineyard had some very old vines, but they had been neglected and the rest of the land was being prepared for new vines. It was vast. It was agreed that I should start the following Monday, despite still not knowing how I would get there and back. In the end, Bill drove me there and arranged to pick me up each evening. It meant leaving the house at 6.45 a.m., so I would have to leave the children their uniforms and breakfasts ready, and trust that they got off to school OK. I did put some responsibility on Martin, putting him in charge. I left lists for the kids to follow – I really thought that it wouldn't be for long.

The first morning, turning up at the vineyard, I met the other ladies, who were all Australians. The other workers included the foreman, who was a miserable-looking devil, Swampy the tractor, Neil the young labourer and Old Jim, who knew everything there was to know about the land and was really only there for the pocket money. I was glad that it was September – it was warm but not stinking hot. Old Jim insisted on calling me 'pommie bastard', but I found out that with Jim, it was almost a term of endearment, and that I shouldn't be offended. In any case, I wasn't there to be offended – I was there for the money, plain and simple. We were divided into three groups, with one male to each group of women. I was put with a young woman called Josie, and Old Jim was our mentor. Josie was not much used to physical work – to be truthful, she was not used to work at all. She had not been married very long, and she and her husband were living with her parents until their house was ready. The owner of the vineyard was a Mr Gursansky, and he lived on the property with his wife and four small daughters.

The job entailed running bell wire (which is extremely tough galvanised wire) along the wooden posts which the men had put into the ground at intervals along the rows in which the vines were to be planted. Old Jim carried the big roll of wire and, as we walked down the rows, we were to nail staples in to fix the wire to the posts. At the other end of the row, Jim would tighten the length of wire so that it was taut. Tighten it too much and there would be a twang and the wire would fly round and could take your eye out. It didn't happen very often, as Jim knew what he was doing. It wasn't too hard a job apart from it being monotonous, but things were to get much harder in the near future.

We all met up at lunch break, which we took in the middle of the vineyard. The other women were a jolly bunch. Two in particular were real characters, Thelma and Vida, whose language was very colourful and whose favourite word was 'jeez'. One good thing that came out of the lunchtime conversation was that I found out that Josie lived not too far away from me; she offered to give me a lift to work and back home again. That was good news and I was sure Bill would be very pleased about that.

We were warned to watch out for snakes and spiders, especially when working in the established vines, where you could not see if there was anything lurking in the undergrowth. After the first week, two ladies dropped out – fortunately for me, Josie was not one of them.

At the end of October, I had a letter from one of my friends. I had written to her voicing my frustration at the lack of success in locating our furniture. She suggested that I should try contacting the Action Line in one of the national newspapers – what a brilliant idea! I immediately wrote to the newspaper, outlining all the information that I thought they might need, including dates and so on. For the first time in ages I felt optimistic.

The weather was getting quite hot, and I came home from

work one day to find that the whole worktop in the kitchen was a seething mass of ants. There was one continuous line coming into the kitchen and another line going back out. When I checked the source of the attraction, I found that one of the kids had poured a glass of juice and dripped a bit on to the worktop. That was enough of a signal to every ant within a five-mile radius to converge on our kitchen. It was a hard lesson, but we learned that we had to keep everything in the fridge; if anything was spilled it had to be wiped up immediately. We couldn't keep anything sugary in the cupboard, and anything containing flour would end up being infested with weevils. All wildlife seemed to be more aggressive in Australia. Gauze was fitted on every window and door to stop the flies from getting in, although they would sometimes sneak in on someone's back. They didn't lay eggs but maggots, so you had to be very careful not to leave any food uncovered. White ants or termites were also prevalent, and one night we were awakened by the sound of munching. Bill tracked the noise down to a corner of the bedroom. Removing the strip of beading from the corner, we found thousands of white ants having the time of their lives. They also attacked the door jamb in the kitchen, and we discovered them when the door fell off – they had eaten everything except the paint. Apparently the house had been neglected while it was standing empty; weatherboard houses were supposed to be treated annually by the flick man, but that hadn't happened on our house. When we got the pest exterminator out to deal with our problem, he found the biggest termite mound underneath the house that he had ever seen.

In the back garden there was a huge swing, easily big enough for an adult. Each morning, very early, two kookaburras would come and sit on each end of the top posts and make the most terrific din. They weren't called laughing jackasses for nothing – but one thing was for sure, we never needed an alarm clock. Rosellas would fly around in the tall trees that surrounded our house; they were a type of parrot. We could also hear the sound of bellbirds. They actually made a sound like hundreds of bells ringing. A new suburb that was being built just outside Cessnock was named Bellbird – there were some beautiful new houses springing up. On the whole, Australian people were friendly; if

Diamonds in the Coal Dust

they passed you in the street, the greeting would be 'G'day, how are ye?' They weren't really asking the question, they didn't really want to know, it was just the common greeting for Aussies.

Our circle of friends began to grow, mainly as a result of the children and their friends at school. The weather had started to warm up considerably and whereas I had been going to work in trousers and a top, stripping off as the day wore on, now I was in shorts and a top, progressing to a smaller top and straw hat, and still the sun became hotter. We were always glad when we made it to the end of a row, where our drink bottles were hanging, just to be able to wet our lips. When we went to work, we would be equipped with insulated bottles – the bigger the better – and they would be filled with orange juice topped up with ice. Through the course of the day the ice would have melted, making ice-cold orange juice – a life saver.

One day, Thelma and Vida suggested that Bill and I visited their stomping ground on the following Saturday night. There was to be some function or other on at the club. Bill said that it would make a change, as I didn't normally go out on a Saturday. When we arrived at the club, I couldn't see either of them, but I suddenly heard a yell: 'Hey, Maddie, over here – jeez, I didn't know you with your clothes on!' That set the tone of the evening. It seemed a lively place; everybody was dancing and you weren't allowed to sit out. An elderly man came along and swept me up. My feet were nearly off the ground – I was glad when the music stopped. In the interval, there was a drum roll and a full Scottish pipe band came marching in; the noise was deafening. They looked a handsome sight in their kilts and regalia, and I suddenly noticed Vida get up and make her way among the swirling kilts. I couldn't believe my eyes as she started to crawl round the floor, looking under the kilts of the men. Everyone was laughing, so they were obviously used to her antics. It was a laugh, and both Bill and I really enjoyed the evening.

Some weeks after my letter to the newspaper in England, I received some wonderful news: our stuff had been located, still on the docks in Tilbury – the haulage company had said that they had not had a container big enough to send everything together. Somebody had obviously cocked up big-time, but the good news was that it was now on its way and would be with us on 2 December. I was so grateful to the Action Line as I think that without their intervention we would never have got anywhere. I couldn't believe it – after all those months of roughing it and sleeping on the floor, we would be civilised again – it would be marvellous to have our own linen – and the arrival of the washing machine would mean I wouldn't have to wash out by hand any longer – pure luxury. We tried to remember what else there was in the packing case, but we couldn't.

The weather by now was extremely hot, and the children were going round in T-shirts and shorts, bare-footed. Nicola looked like a fair dinkem Aussie; her hair, which was already fair, was now almost white, and she had a lovely tan, as we all had. Nicola had a friend called Jan Patrick, a big girl. She lived not too far away from us and she had a horse called Bubs. Several of her own friends had horses, and it became the norm for them all to come to our property on their horses after school, as we had lots of open space plus the two paddocks. They made their own jumps with pieces of wood and oil drums. Most of them rode bareback and bare-foot. It wasn't too long before Nicola started asking if she could have a horse. We held out for a while and then started thinking about the possibility. We didn't know anything about horses, but Bill asked a few questions at work. One of the young men there said he would help us out with advice and do any shoeing that was needed. We were looking out for a suitable horse, and spotted what looked like a suitable one, not too far from where we lived. He was a bit big for a beginner – at 14 hands high – but Nicola's friend assured us that she would be able to handle it, as she had been riding their different horses without any trouble. We went to look at Star, a chestnut gelding; he looked a bit of a handful to me. We said that we would think about it for a few days, but I think we knew that it was going to be a sale. Nicola was very excited. We went into Cessnock and got her kitted out with the basics: brushes, bridle, hay, bucket and goodness knows what else. The previous owner was bringing Star in his transporter, and everyone was excited except me – I was apprehensive. Nicola's friends were going to be there for the arrival, so there was quite a reception committee. When he appeared out of the transporter, he had a good look round and then wandered off to munch the grass. We decided to let him have the freedom of the property, as it was completely fenced off. We would never need to use the lawnmower again! Each morning, Nicola would brush him and make sure he had fresh water, and as soon as she came home from school, she was on his back. She was fearless. Most of the other kids would swap their horses – Nicola expected to do the same, except that none of the others would ride Star. But Nicola didn't mind.

We had finished putting the wires in for the new vines, and it would soon be time to harvest the grapes from the established vines. It was extremely hot – over 100 degrees in the sun at midday. Josie had decided that the work was too much for her and left. I was faced with a dilemma as to how I could get to work and home again. I had a word with the boss and he suggested that I get a lift with the foreman, who lived in Cessnock. It meant me walking into Cessnock to the pick-up point and being dropped there at home time. I don't think that the foreman was particularly pleased to do me the favour, as he never made conversation with me, but I wasn't bothered. The manager took on extra staff for the grape picking, as there was only a narrow window for them to be harvested. Plenty of fluids were needed to keep us going; the work was not only very exhausting but, with the extreme heat, one could very quickly become dehydrated. The pickers would move down the rows with secateurs, snipping the bunches of grapes and dropping them into buckets. When your bucket was full, it had to be emptied into a trailer on the back of the tractor which moved slowly down the rows to be emptied into the trailer. It rained heavily one weekend. I had Wellingtons on my feet but the mud sucked me down, especially when I had the weight of a full bucket, and, more often than not, I ended up leaving my wellies behind in the mud. It was easier to work barefoot. After two days, two of the grape pickers left – one finished up in hospital with heatstroke and the other just could not hack it. I stuck it out through the grape picking, and then we had a month off – oh, bliss!

On 1 December we were notified that our things would be arriving the next day. I don't think we slept that night! I was alone when the furniture van pulled up; the kids were at school and Bill was at work. The men carried the furniture in, but the very large packing case had to be left on the veranda, as it was too large to fit through the double doors. I set about going through the house deciding where everything would go. There was certainly enough room for everything. My dining room suite looked good in the living room and I chucked the mattress out of our bedroom to make way for our bed; it was so exciting. The washing machine was installed in the laundry room – no more washing out by hand! I left the packing case to be opened when the kids and Bill came home.

It was just like Christmas. It was so long since it had been packed that we had forgotten just what was in there. Bill was ecstatic when his fishing tackle was unearthed, I was pleased to get my hands on my own bed linen and kitchen equipment, and the children were just happy to be reunited with their favourite things from home, things they had thought they would never see again. Curtains were put up and pictures hung on the walls; it felt more like home now.

Christmas was fast approaching – our first Christmas away from home. In Australia, it was the summer holidays, and most Aussies moved to the coast for three weeks, Nicola's friend Jan was going with her family to Blacksmiths Beach. They took a tent and most of their possessions, and invited Nicola to go with them; however, I wanted us to have a proper English Christmas all together. I must admit that the kids didn't seem to have got as much in the way of presents as usual, simply because most of our relatives had sent money in lieu of presents. We put up the tree, which we had brought from home, and decorated the room, but it just didn't seem right. I put the turkey in the oven and did the veggies, but by 11 a.m. the temperature had climbed to over 100 degrees and every fly for miles around was hanging on the gauze doors waiting for an invite to come in. Bill said, 'Turn the oven off, we're off to the beach. We'll have dinner tonight.' I didn't need to be told twice. We packed a few things for Nicola and went off to find her friend in Blacksmiths.

It was wonderful on the coast – not much cooler, but with the sea breeze it was much more bearable. Everybody was busy with a barbecue; I couldn't believe it. They had taken table and chairs, even the fridge – it was like home from home. We left Nicola with Jan and her family, and said that we would pick her up the following week, and then we went home to cook our Christmas dinner. We learned that first Christmas that tradition was all very well, but concessions had to be made for the weather.

On New Year's Eve, we had been invited to Monica and George's house. As Monica was babysitting her young grandson, she said that she would do a buffet – we were to go to the club with George, and then back to their house in time to see the New Year in. Monica's Jan had gone off with her boyfriend, but they were also coming before midnight. We returned about 11 p.m. and found that Monica had done us proud. There was a mountain of savouries, and a lovely iced New Year cake that George had won in a raffle, and of course plenty of bubbly. Jan and her boyfriend returned just in time, and it was decided that he would let the New Year in at midnight. Three minutes before midnight, he went outside with the family black cat, a piece of coal and a shiny new fifty-cent piece. The chimes struck and we all sung Auld Lang Syne, but there was no sign of Jan's man. When we opened the door, he was on his hands and knees – the cat had scratched him, he had dropped the cat, followed by the coal, followed by the fifty-cent piece. It was a laugh and an unforgettable night.

After the holidays, things returned to normal, whatever that was. Nicola was to move to the high school which Martin attended. She already had friends there, and she threw herself into the different activities which were on offer. She joined the music society, the choir and the dramatic society. Martin's big love was still football; he didn't seem to want to join anything else, although he had formed one or two relationships with lads in our neck of the woods. He was invited to play for the rugby team and quite enjoyed it. But, in only his second game, he received a bad knock which quickly put paid to his fledgling rugby career. He came home from the match on his bike, dragging one leg. His knee was very swollen and he couldn't bend it, so I said that he should stay home from school and rest the leg. When I arrived home from work the next day, it was obvious that things were far from right. When Bill came home, I asked him to take Martin and me to the doctor. Dr Fuller was very concerned and prescribed very strong antibiotics with instructions for Martin to stay off the leg. He had a raging temperature and wasn't aware of what was going on. The next day the appearance of his leg had changed; the drugs were working and an abscess was forming where the poison was being drawn out. One day later and the abscess had burst, much to Martin's relief and ours, too, I might say. When he was able to hobble, we took him back to the doctor, who told us in no uncertain terms how lucky Martin had been. 'He could have lost his leg,' he said. 'No more rugby for you.' After a couple of weeks, Martin was back to his normal self, but the abscess had left quite a large hole in his leg. It didn't stop him playing soccer, though.

Back in the vineyard, my next task was pruning. By this time I was the only female working there – I don't know whether I was lucky or just plain crackers. Fortunately the men didn't seem to mind me being there or the fact that I was a Pom, but they did try to wind me up. They would insist on trying to copy my Yorkshire accent, with not much success. Old Jim took me under his wing, and made sure that I was doing the job right, but they didn't make any concessions for the fact that I was female – I was expected to keep up with the men. The weather was still very hot and we had to be continually aware of the dangers of snakes. These weren't so noticeable when we were a gang of chattering women, as they would prefer to keep out of the way, but working my way down a row of vines quietly on my own, it was easy to disturb a snake, and that was dangerous.

Whoever named Swampy did a good job, as the name suited him down to the ground. He was not pretty and he always looked as if he had got out of bed as he got in, and vice versa. If he drove the tractor down one of the rows and disturbed a snake, he would shout 'snake!', grab a spanner and chase it closely, followed by the other workers – all except me, as I headed in the other direction. I didn't escape entirely, though, as Swampy would nail the dead snake to the end post of the row I would be working in next. I wasn't frightened of dead ones, only the ones which could bite me. Swampy could grab a snake by the tail, crack it like a whip

Diamonds in the Coal Dust

and it would be dead instantly… or so he said. I could not let my nerves get the better of me or I would have had to pack the job in, and I wasn't about to do that.

I had a little leather pouch in which I carried my secateurs and my other tools of the trade, and at the end of each day I would hang the bag on the post of the row I was due to work on the next morning. One such morning, I picked up my bag and fastened it round my waist. When I took my secateurs out, I found that I had a visitor. I screamed and Old Jim came to see what the fuss was about. 'Jeez, it's a bloody redback,' he said. Apparently a redback spider is quite deadly. I learned an important lesson that day; always check before sticking your hand in anywhere. The men thought it was hilarious. The funnel web spider is also very dangerous, as apparently it will jump at you if it feels threatened.

I always made sure that I had enough fluids to drink to last me until home time. I didn't feel much like eating with my mucky hands, but I had to keep drinking. Sometimes it was a close thing making my drinks spin out, especially when it was very hot and dusty. But one particular day, I couldn't wait for home time, and I had finished the last of my bottled juice twenty minutes before. I felt as if I was burning up, and my tongue was sticking to the roof of my mouth. I didn't speak all the way home in the foreman's truck. When he dropped me off in Cessnock, I really didn't know how I was going to make it home. However, I groggily made my way down past the school and on towards the pit yard. Walking through the dust, I saw a small pool of water. I took my hankie and dabbed it in the water then held it to my face. It felt so good. I did this several times and it refreshed me enough to continue on my way home. When I arrived home, Martin burst out laughing. 'What have you been doing?' he asked. 'You look as though you've got war paint on.' When I looked in the mirror, my face was streaked all over with coal dust, but I didn't care. I think that I drank about three pints of water almost non-stop. After that experience, I always made sure that I had drinks to spare, especially while it was so hot.

Before we moved to Australia, I had been in touch with a girl whom I knew from our village. Daphne was a year older than me and she once went out with a friend of Bill's. His name was Jack and he was a real jack-the-lad. We had been out in a foursome a couple of times years ago. Daphne joined the forces when she was eighteen, and was serving abroad when she met a fellow in the Australian Air Force. She married Don and moved to Australia, to his hometown. When we were thinking about moving to Australia, I got Daphne's address from her family and wrote to her, asking how she had settled in and if she had any regrets. She had two children and loved it, but she did say that it wasn't for everybody. But she had lived there almost fifteen years and considered herself an Aussie, and, of course, her children were true Aussies. There were things that she missed, but she considered she was better off than she would have been in England. After we had been in Australia a few months, she invited us to go and see them for the weekend – they lived in Canberra at this time. Bill thought it might be a good idea to buy a more reliable car, as the journey would take us the better part of a day. He chose a VW estate car; it looked really nice. Martin chose not to come with us, as he had a football match, so he was going to keep an eye on the horse. George and Bill gave the car a going-over and George agreed it was a nice motor. 'You will be OK with that – no worries,' he said. 'No worries' was a phrase we used many times in the future, when we meant that we damn well did have worries. But we set off in high spirits, looking forward to our new adventure.

We had been travelling about four hours when things began to go wrong – the engine appeared to be overheating. We decided to stop for a meal, giving the car engine a chance to cool down. We set off again, but the same thing happened, and we virtually limped into Canberra, where Daphne was waiting for us. Don was still at the office. It was so nice to meet up again, but this was not the Daphne that I remembered. She had married and brought up her family in Australia, and to all intents and purposes, she was Australian. Of course, her two children were true blue Aussie, having been born there. Our kids got on like a house on fire with Daphne's two and, when Don had arrived home, we all felt comfortable. He was a lovely man and suggested that Bill took the car to a local garage to get it looked at. We left the car there, arranging to pick it up the next day.

Diamonds in the Coal Dust

As Don worked most of the weekend, it was left to Daphne to show us round the city of Canberra. Actually it was quite a boring place, having been created by the government for the government as the capital of Australia. It was laid out in squares, all very clean and modern, but sterile somehow, with not a lot of character. We really enjoyed our weekend, talking about old times and home, and it seemed to fly by; however, we promised to keep in touch and the children said that they would write to each other.

When we picked the car up, the mechanic said that he had given it a going-over and replaced a component, and gave us a bill for $175.

We set off for home, poorer but in good humour. It was late afternoon and we thought we would travel into the night, when it would be cooler. One hour out of Canberra, the car died, and we were in the middle of nowhere. We waited a while to see if another vehicle came along, but no such luck. Bill decided to set off to find a telephone or a property where he could get help. He was gone a long time and it was beginning to get dark. Around an hour later he returned, after finding a house where the owner let him use the telephone. He had contacted a garage and they were sending a breakdown vehicle to us. Eventually it arrived and we were all loaded into the front of the breakdown truck, and the car was towed behind us to the garage. When we arrived at the garage, of course, it was closed. The tow truck man told us we would have to wait until morning. The garage was slap bang in the middle of nowhere – no four-star hotel, even if we could have afforded it. Fortunately, we had drinks and snacks with us which we had packed for our journey so there were no problems there. Bill let the back seats down and the girls were able to lie down and go to sleep in the back. Children always seem to adapt to unusual situations and cope better than grown-ups. Bill reclined his seat and managed to catnap; he could have slept on a clothes-line. Me – I sat upright in my seat all night, feeling sorry for myself as usual. It was a long night, but worse was to come, for when the garage eventually opened, the mechanic checked the car and informed Bill that the engine was shot, and it needed a new one. We were devastated – it would be two days, even if they could get a new one or a reconditioned one. We had no option but to phone Daphne and throw ourselves on their good nature again. She came and collected us and took us back to Canberra, but we were also worried about Martin who was expecting us home. There was not a lot we could do, as we were not on the phone in Cessnock. We had to ring the bank in order to transfer the money for the car repair. I cannot say we enjoyed the rest of our stay, as we were so worried. We had given the garage Daphne's phone number, and they were to ring us there when the car was ready. They pulled out all the stops and the phone call came in two days. Don took us to pick it up – I don't know what we would have done without him and Daphne. We went on our way with our new engine, and a much depleted bank account, with no more mishaps.

I was proud to find that Martin had managed very well on his own, but he had wondered what had happened to us. Shortly after our visit, Don was transferred with his family to Hong Kong for two years, so we did not see them again.

Nicola's circle of friends grew, and our place after school sometimes resembled the Ponderosa with all the horses. For myself, I still was not too impressed with Star, and kept my distance as much as possible. If I went into Cessnock for the shopping and got a cab back, I would approach the gate carefully, and was always pleased if I could not see the horse. Sometimes I swear he knew when the cab dropped me off – he would come trotting round, and woe betide me if I was carrying a loaf of bread, as he would grab it off me. Sometimes I would make it to the veranda, and run to the kitchen door; that wouldn't stop him, though, as he would hop on the veranda. Once, the double doors of the kitchen were open. He walked in, walked round the table, had a look to see what was on it and then walked out again. He was a real character. We used to get our milk delivered in a litre polythene bag, which the milkman would leave at the gate, but if he left it on the inside of the gate, the next morning we would find a soggy bit of polythene, as Star would stamp on it and burst it.

I worried about Martin, as he did not seem to be too interested in anything much except his football, although he did go on a skiing holiday from school. But he made no bones about it – he was going home in two years' time. If you were sponsored to go to Australia, and you returned before two years, you had to repay the cost of your flight to the sponsors. To be truthful, with all the mishaps we had experienced since arriving in Australia, I wasn't too sure myself if it had been the right decision to go out there. It wasn't so much the little things that went wrong, or indeed the big ones either, but the fact that you didn't have a shoulder to cry on nor anyone to share your troubles with. Nobody cared a damn; if you had a little gripe, all you would get in reply would be, 'Well, what did you come for?' Which I suppose was a fair comment.

We had kept in touch with Chris and Mona in Wollongong, and we invited them to come and stay with us for a few days. The weekend that they were coming, Bill wasn't due home until 8 p.m. They arrived in the middle of the afternoon. Chris said, 'I don't believe it, we pulled up in the main street of Cessnock and asked somebody whether they knew Bill Worth and they did.' They had directed him to our property. Chris said that Bill was better known than the bell ringer. I myself could not believe how broad Yorkshire Chris sounded; we hadn't heard anybody from Yorkshire speak for over a year. I said to him, 'Do we sound as broad as you?' He said that we did, but I couldn't believe that. It was nice to spend some time with someone from home, and, when Bill arrived home, he and Chris had a real old chinwag, each one trying to outdo the other. We took them all round our area, including the vineyard where I worked. Obviously, that one wasn't open for business, but we visited the others in the vicinity, where they got the chance to sample plenty of the local plonk. They also bought plenty to take back with them, as it was so inexpensive. I got plenty of chances to ask Mona what she thought about Australia. She admitted that she was desperately lonely and homesick, even though they had their family and also owned a car, which was something that they had never had in England. I did appreciate how she felt – if I hadn't had my job, I don't know what I would have done.

It seems strange that if Bill had taken the job in Wollongong we would have been living quite close to them, but you never can be quite sure which is the right decision; you just have to go for it and hope for the best – more importantly, don't have any regrets. Chris and Mona were in the process of moving into an apartment, and invited us to stay with them after their move. I felt a bit sad when they left us, as we had really enjoyed their company, but we promised that it wouldn't be long before we saw them again.

My job at the vineyard didn't get any easier except for the fact that it was much cooler now. Monica and George were feeling the pinch, as George wasn't getting any bonus at work, and they were looking after their little grandson and also had their son to put through school. I suggested that Monica came to work with me at the vineyard. She wasn't too keen on the idea, but my argument was that if you needed money, you couldn't be too proud. I enquired at work as to whether they would give her a job and they asked me if she was a good worker. I had to say that I did not know. 'OK, we will give her a try,' said the boss. When I told Monica, I thought that she would be over the moon, but she wasn't. However, she turned up on the Monday morning, a great big straw hat almost enveloping her. I introduced her to the boss and to Old Jim – I could tell he was giving her the once-over. So off we went. She was supplied with secateurs, and I was told to show her the ropes. I soon learned that she was not happy with the set-up. She would say, 'I am not going down there, they can't make us – we can't see if there are any snakes.' I couldn't believe it, as I had worked there so long – yes, I was scared of snakes and spiders, but I just kept my head down and hoped for the best. I hadn't been bitten so far. I knew that Monica was not going to cut the mustard, as she kept saying, 'If my girls in the typing pool could see me now…' I felt like saying, 'I am sure that they would be very proud of you.' At lunchtime, Old Jim asked us how things were going. I said, 'OK.' Monica, however, launched into a tirade of how women should not be expected to go alone where it was dangerous. Old Jim took me on one side and said that she was a whinging Pom b—d. Not a good start. On the fourth day, she didn't turn up. By that time, I had myself got a bit fed up of 'If my girls could see me now'. Old Jim asked me where the whinging Pom was, and I said that I didn't think she was coming any more. 'Thank God,' he said. With the Aussies, you did have to earn your stripes. Bill experienced it at his workplace also. But once you were accepted, you were OK.

When things were a bit quiet in the vineyard, I was sent to pick strawberries. Mr Gursansky had a sizeable patch, quite near the house. It was on a slope overlooking one of the dams which were used for irrigation. If anything, it was worse than the vines, as snakes tended to be drawn to water and, as the strawberries were on the floor, you couldn't always see just where you were putting your hands. But it was more pleasant, as at lunchtime I could shelter from the elements in one of the outbuildings. The family had a couple of cats which were always about. I once saw one of the cats being chased by a bird – obviously it had strayed too close to the nest. But I was also told that the same cat had caught a snake and killed it.

Every two years around Cessnock they had the Hunter Valley Vintage Festival. This was a kind of showcase for the different vineyards to advertise their own wines. The festival was held on the showground in Cessnock, with each vineyard or winery having its own marquee. These were huge affairs, in different shapes; one was in the shape of a castle. Visitors to the festival could purchase a commemorative wine glass at the entrance, and a reel of tickets – each time you wished to sample a particular wine, you would give up one of your tickets. Monica and I, with Ann in tow, set off in one direction, Bill and George in the other. It was a lovely warm sunny day, and there was a lovely happy atmosphere, helped no doubt by the many samples of wine which were quaffed. Each time our glasses were filled, Ann would say, 'Can I try that?' in turn to Monica and me. We were walking round the showground, all three of us with arms linked, when I became aware that Ann was acting strangely. She was talking a bit funny, and swaying a bit. I was so embarrassed when I realised that she was getting squiffy. I set off to find her dad. We wasted no time in getting her into the car and taking her home. She was put to bed, where she was to stay until the evening, in time to go and join the crowds in the main street for the big parade of floats carrying the Vintage Queen and her entourage, plus the floats which entered from different businesses in the town. The finale was a firework display, and a happy end to a most memorable day, not least because of Ann having had a little too much to drink.

Chapter Four

After our second Christmas in Australia, Martin began to make serious noises about returning to England. We would have been in Australia for two years the following June, and Martin would be sixteen. He was very intelligent, but he just didn't seem to have any high aspirations at Cessnock. I had to admit that Cessnock was not exactly the place for a high flier to spread his wings. We decided that he could go back to his old school, and possibly take his GCSEs. He would be able to stay with Bill's mum and dad, who lived quite near the school. We ourselves had talked about going home. Nicola didn't want to, Ann did. It wasn't all bad, but future prospects for the children seemed to be a bit limited. The quality of life was not as great as we felt it should have been for the effort we were putting in. Cessnock itself was a bit of a one-horse town – perhaps we expected too much, perhaps if we had gone to a different part of Australia it might have been different – who knows?

We booked Martin on a flight for the beginning of July; it seemed like a long way off.

Nicola always had something on at school. She was learning to play the flute, and had a leading part in the school play, *Noyes Flud*. She rehearsed the words and songs so much that I think that I could have taken the part myself. In her spare time she also had her horse, of course.

As the time drew nearer for Martin to leave us, I became more and more nervous – how could I let one of my kids go to the other side of the world on his own, not knowing when we would see him again? We had a heated debate and the decision was made: we would follow in the near future.

As I said, Bill liked to go off fishing with his mates for the weekend. They would load up the fishing tackle and the all-important keg of beer. One Sunday evening, he came home with

Diamonds in the Coal Dust

the cooler box full of prawns; they were huge king prawns and delicious. We had some for supper and put the rest in the freezer. Some things in Australia were super. Bill, I think, would miss his fishing/drinking mates.

I didn't mention the fact that I might be going home to the boss at the vineyard – I didn't feel it was necessary, and also I thought it might not be received too well. Bill decided not to tell them at his workplace either, until it was nearer the time. The family back home were thrilled at the idea of Martin going home and even more so when we told them that we were planning on going back as well. My aunt was especially pleased at the news; she was not getting any younger and, I think, was not getting out much.

Chris and Mona had been urging us to go and see them, so we decided to tell them we would go after Martin went home. They were surprised to learn about Martin – I didn't know what they would say when we told them we were also thinking of following him.

As Martin's leaving day came nearer, he had a few farewell dos with school friends. There was a debs' ball and Martin was an escort for one of the young ladies; he wasn't too keen on the idea, but all the sixteen-year-olds were expected to escort one of the 'debs'. It wasn't much in Martin's line. A week before he was due to fly home, he said one evening that he wasn't sure if he wanted to go. That put the cat among the pigeons, and we tried to find out what had changed his mind. He wasn't sure. However, after toing and froing for a day or two, he decided he would go after all. We took him to the airport in Sydney. I felt quite anxious, although Martin didn't seem too phased. We struck up a conversation with a gentleman who was going on the same flight, and he said that he would keep an eye on Martin, who was sensible and used to travelling on his own to various football matches. We stayed at the airport until the plane was just a dot in the sky, then drove home in silence. It would be strange without my son, but we had a plan of our own to make.

The following week, we went to Wollongong to see Chris and Mona. We loved where they lived, a first-floor flat halfway up Mount Keira. The balcony overlooked Wollongong harbour, which at night was a magical sight. The ships which were anchored in the harbour were lit up in the darkness, and looking down on it all was like looking at the illuminations back home.

Mona was still very homesick, and when we told them that we were planning on going home, it unsettled her even more. I thought that they were quite lucky to live where they did, but it doesn't help when you are missing home so much. I thought that as they had family out there, it would have been easier for her, but she said not.

I do think that if we had gone to Wollongong when we first went out, it might have been easier to settle, but who knows? As we went round the town, we thought it was gorgeous. It was on the coast, and they could walk down into the town to some very nice shops. Chris suggested that Bill could easily get a job in the pit in Wollongong. Perhaps if we had upped sticks when we first came to Australia and moved down there, we might have settled. Now, it was too late – our son had already gone, and we had made the decision to follow him.

The first morning that we were there, we set off to explore. It was all downhill into town, and there was one long street, but the difference between Wollongong and Cessnock were the shops – very modern, very plentiful and very tempting. At the end of the long street was the beach, miles of it with nobody on it. We had lunch in one of the many cafés and then it was off to the hypermarket just outside town. It was massive – there was nothing like that in Cessnock. Mona had acquired a taste for Aussie wine, and you could buy a five-litre pack for next to nothing. Chris and Bill of course stocked up on the amber nectar. The next morning after breakfast, we took a picnic and went up Mount Keira. There was a place with tables and benches, where you could have a barbecue. Later in the day we called to see Chris and Mona's daughter and her husband and their two children. They loved life in Australia, and had lots of friends. I think that the difference between them and us was the fact that their little girl was just a toddler when they went out there, and the little boy was actually born out there. Our children, on the other hand, were probably the wrong age to uproot and move lock, stock and barrel – although Nicola had adapted well, so perhaps it was just down to temperament. We

Diamonds in the Coal Dust

really enjoyed our stay in Wollongong, and left Chris and Mona, promising to keep in touch.

Things moved quite quickly after we returned to Cessnock. We decided we would go at the end of September, so that the girls would not miss much of the new school year in England. We decided to make our journey home a bit of a holiday, and booked our passage on a ship sailing from Sydney to Singapore; we would then fly from Singapore to London. We booked one cabin with four berths, on a good deck and with a porthole. The fares actually cost the same as the air fares would have done if we were flying. Once we had decided when we were going, it seemed easier somehow. We looked on the rest of our stay in Australia as a holiday, even though we were still working. At weekends, we went off on trips to see different sights. We went into Sydney and saw the Opera House and the harbour; it was bustling with people from all sorts of countries as sightseers. Another weekend we went to Gosford to the animal park; there were plenty of koalas and so on, but there were also lots of snakes. They had them to produce the poison which would be made into anti-venom for people who were bitten by snakes. One evening we went for a ride and planned to call for a drink, but on our way back could see smoke in the distance. As we drew nearer, we could see that it was a bush fire. We could feel the heat all around us, but the fire seemed to be up in the tree tops, and the flames were leaping from one tree to the next. It was very scary and we were pleased when we left it behind us.

We had a couple of trips to the vineyards for a 'cheap drink' as George called it, and stocked up with wine. One weekend, we went for a ride to Barrington Tops, which was a lookout over the mountains with spectacular views. We took a picnic with us. Nicola stayed with Jan to ride her horse. Monica brought her grandson Shaughn, and her son Ian also came along; we, of course, had Ann with us. We had a super day, sitting on a blanket; the weather was glorious.

I finally decided to tell my boss at the vineyard that I would be leaving the following week, to give me a chance to organise what we were taking home and what we had to dispose of. We were only taking back what would fit into the packing case, which was still sitting on the back veranda. The men at my workplace took it well, but Old Jim was quite sarcastic and wanted to know what the heck I wanted to go back to a dump like England for. I didn't bother quantifying my reasons, and told him that I might be back one day. I believe he said, 'We won't let you in again.' He didn't mean to be so obnoxious – he was just a crusty old Aussie. Bill was not telling the boss at the pit until the last minute, as we wouldn't be leaving the house until the day before our departure. We found a buyer for Star. I felt so sorry for Nicola, as she loved that horse to bits, but we were assured that he was going to a good home.

The furniture and car were sold with the proviso that we would keep them until the last minute. I worked at the vineyard for a further week and Bill worked his notice. His boozing mates had a bit of a do for him and presented him with a pewter tankard, bearing the message 'To Bill from George's P P club'. Bill was really touched by their gesture, and promised to keep the tankard, which he did.

The man who bought Star came to collect him with a horse box, and Star did not want to go in it. It was very upsetting for Nicola, having to say goodbye to him. Nicola's friends had umpteen leaving dos for her, and there were lots of tears.

Looking back, it did not seem two years since we had arrived. Martin and Nicola had grown into adults while we were there, and even Ann had grown up.

We had fun with the packing case. Bill was determined that all his fishing tackle should be packed, and the kids had their own ideas as to what should go and what should be left. Ann had acquired a bike one Christmas, so that had to be packed. The linen and crockery that we brought out with us was not going back. We did not know where we would be living, so decided that we would have a fresh start. The case was collected a couple of days before we left; it would be held in England until we notified them as to where we needed it to be delivered.

The night before we were due to sail, George picked us up and took us to their house, where we were to spend the last night. The grown-ups didn't sleep much that night; we sat up and talked and talked. I promised Monica that we would keep in touch. She

Diamonds in the Coal Dust

said that as soon as we got home we would forget all about them, but I never did.

We travelled on the train to Sydney, and we all had our own private thoughts. Were we doing the right thing? What was the right thing? Decisions are made and you have to stand by those decisions; some of them may be right, some of them may be wrong – so what?

We got a cab to the harbour, and found our ship. It was huge – I had never seen anything like it. We were not due to embark until 1 p.m., so we went and had lunch and a last look round. We then checked our luggage and our passports in, and were welcomed on board and shown to our cabin. It was like a dream, very exciting – even Nicola seemed to have cheered up.

We were just tidying ourselves up when there was a knock on the door of the cabin. Nicola went to answer it and we were surprised to see Monica standing there. She had come to see us off. We had not known that visitors were allowed on board, but apparently they could stay until one and half hours before sailing. It was sad saying goodbye again, but it was a lovely thought of Monica's. We had an hour together, and then an announcement was made for all visitors to disembark. Monica said that she would wave to us from the quay. We went up on the top deck and there was an amazing sight – hundreds of people watching and waving from the observation platform. Some of them had brought lines and lines of tights all knotted together; one end was tied to the handrail of the ship and the other was held by the spectators. We spotted Monica waving to us all by herself, and I felt so sad. The ship's hooter sounded and we were off, dragging a trail of streamers and tights behind us. We waved until we couldn't see anybody any more. As we rounded the harbour, we sailed under Sydney Harbour Bridge, and there was the Opera House. It was lit up by this time, as dusk was falling. What an unforgettable sight... the fiery red of the setting sun and the bright lights of Sydney fading away behind us.

We just had time to change for the evening meal, which was the only downside of the trip – well, one of them. As Ann was under eleven years of age, she was not allowed to eat in the restaurant; she had to dine with the littlies. For the first couple of mealtimes I went with her and stayed until she had finished, but she soon became friendly with the other children, and they would all go off quite happily by themselves. After the children had eaten, they would then go to the playroom, where they were entertained while their parents ate.

The food in the restaurant was superb, and Bill, Nicola and I shared a table with a Scottish couple who were returning home with their three young children. Over the course of the journey, we became quite friendly with them, and when I received an invitation to their cabin, I was amazed. It was two decks below ours, and the heat and the throbbing of the engines was almost unbearable. I hadn't realised that the position of the cabin and which deck you were on could make such a difference. I don't think that I could have stood it down there.

Our first stop was Melbourne, and we were allowed to go ashore for a few hours. We went on one of the famous tram cars for a short ride. The weather was not too good – I think Melbourne is known for its inclement weather – but it was nice to see yet another part of Australia. None of us had been affected by sea sickness, but sailing round the Great Australian Bight, we hit some very rough weather. Sick bags appeared – tucked behind the hand rails along the corridors. The restaurant became fairly quiet as more and more passengers succumbed to the dreaded mal de mer. The curtains in the dining room were kept shut, but sitting in the lounge you could watch the bow of the ship rise and fall.

Margaret and Robbie (the Scottish couple) had a seven-year-old daughter, and one day she was a little off-colour; they weren't too alarmed until she came out in spots. They took her to see the ship's doctor, who immediately put her in quarantine. It must have been a frightening ordeal for her, on her own in the little hospital. Her mother stayed with her as much as possible and her dad took his turn, but it wasn't ideal. One day when Bill came out in a rash, we feared the worst. He said that there was no chance of him going into quarantine, so he kept his shirt buttoned up to hide the spots on his chest. However, an incident one night changed all that. While we were in Australia, we had found that anything and everything that bites or stings makes a beeline for

Bill. Mosquitoes would climb over me in bed to get to Bill. One night a few days into our journey, Bill was awakened by something that was trying to eat him alive while he was lying on his bunk. He quickly flicked on the light and let out a yell – he was covered in little monsters that were biting him for all they were worth. The light must have disturbed them, as they scuttled down between the mattress and the wall. Bill dragged the mattress off the bed, exposing more of these parasites in the crack between the mattress and the bed frame. The girls were still asleep, blissfully unaware of the drama, when Bill yelled, 'They're bed bugs!' Neither Bill nor I slept any more for the rest of the night. This was obviously the cause of Bill's rash.

First thing next morning, Bill was off to the purser's office, with evidence of his experience – a piece of paper on which lay several dead bugs. The girls and I sat outside the office, while the incident was being investigated. Suddenly, the door flew open and Bill, the purser and two more men strode off down the corridor. Bill shouted to us to stay where we were. After several minutes the procession returned, the purser holding a sheet of paper with several of the offending bugs on it. I had to stop myself from laughing, it really looked so comical. However, we were taken into the office where the purser apologised profusely. His explanation was that the ship had been to Fiji prior to this trip, and the previous occupants of our cabin had bought a grass linen basket. This, he said, must have been the cause of the infestation. We were moved into two separate cabins, which were adjoining; the girls weren't a bit bothered about being on their own. Apparently, the staff threw the mattresses overboard and the cabin was fumigated. As for Bill's rash, we were crossing the equator at the time, so Bill found a quiet spot and sunned himself in private. He was still a bit embarrassed at stripping off his shirt in front of everyone. The strong sun soon cleared up his spots, and he did not have to be quarantined.

When we left Australia, I was in charge of everything of value. I had a shoulder bag which contained passports, birth certificates and all the money we were taking home with us. I was paranoid about keeping hold of the bag, but I did have one very scary incident. On each deck were a laundry room and a separate ironing room. One particular day, I had done the girls' washing and drying, but the ironing room on our deck was already being used, so I set off to look for a vacant one on another deck. I eventually found one, did the job and set off back to our cabin. As soon as I arrived there, I realised that I had left my bag behind the door of the ironing room. I was shaking, and when I told Bill, he called me all the names under the sun, and a few more besides. 'Where have you left it?' he yelled. I didn't stop to answer, but flew out of the cabin.

I couldn't think straight, and didn't even know which deck I had been on. I felt faint with fear. I maniacally dashed up one corridor and down the other. I couldn't go back without it. I looked on every deck. I am sure that anybody seeing me thought I was a mad woman, which I was at the time. Finally, I looked in an empty ironing room and there, sitting behind the door, was my bag. I said a little prayer of thanks before heading back to our cabin, to relay the good news to Bill, who was still foaming at the mouth. He again berated me for being so careless, but I could handle it this time as I had got a good result. I think he would have thrown me overboard if I had not managed to retrieve it.

Anyway, the trip was wonderful, and worth every penny we paid for it, despite our little 'upsets'.

Our cabin boy was a young lad from Singapore, called Jimmy A, and he was nineteen years old. His home was in Singapore, and he told us that when we docked in Singapore, where we would have two days to come and go as we pleased, he would escort us. He advised us not to wander around on our own, as some areas were a bit run-down to put it mildly. A couple of days before we docked, there came an announcement over the tannoy, telling the passengers that any male expecting to go ashore should have their hair checked, as any man with shoulder-length hair would not be allowed ashore.

As we would be flying from Singapore to Gatwick in a couple of days, we were to use the ship as a hotel, but were warned that we had to stick strictly to the laws of the land. Chewing gum was not allowed in the streets, either.

The first morning, as soon as we had finished breakfast, we

Diamonds in the Coal Dust

couldn't wait to go ashore and stretch our legs. We were looking forward to exploring on our own. Jimmy was on duty until after lunch, when he would be escorting us around. The heat and humidity were stifling, and there was a funny smell. It was like nothing we had ever seen before; the streets had gullies running down the sides of the roads, and people were coming out of shacks and emptying slop buckets into the gullies – it was very smelly. The shacks had no glass in the windows, just rolled-up bamboo curtains which presumably they dropped down at nighttime. There were locals with barrows, cooking by the side of the road, and the food was displayed on what looked like dustbin lids. Businessmen in suits were buying whatever was being cooked, and eating as they walked along. There were flies everywhere. Ann was feeling the heat and beginning to flag, and, as I didn't fancy risking food from one of the dodgy barrows, we headed back to our floating hotel.

After lunch, Jimmy sought us out and we told him of our little foray that morning. He told us that we had gone to an area that only locals normally go to. We decided to leave any more sightseeing until the next morning. Jimmy would be at our disposal for the whole of the day, as his term of employment was due to finish that day.

We did most of our packing, so that we could leave our last day completely free. Jimmy took us in an entirely different direction to the one we had staggered through the day before. It was like a different country, with wide, spotlessly clean streets, and big modern gleaming shopping malls. We had obviously seen the worst of Singapore the day before; this was more like it. Jimmy knew exactly where to take us. There were designer shops aplenty, and Jimmy stressed that we should never pay the price that was displayed on any particular item. Not that I could afford anything anyway, but it was good to look. Bill spotted a watch he really fancied, and asked Jimmy to see how cheaply he could get it; he was highly delighted when he came away with it at a price which Jimmy said was a real bargain. He treasured that Seiko watch, even after it no longer worked, which was many years later. We had lunch in a state-of-the-art diner that was spotless. We moved among the many little souvenir shops selling things native to Singapore, looking for a souvenir for Martin, and finally decided on a ceremonial dagger. It was in a scabbard, beautifully carved and with a wicked-looking blade... very unusual.

Wherever you looked, building work was going on, and a monorail was being constructed over the roads. We finished our tour in the Tiger Balm Gardens, which were very impressive, and took some memorable photographs of the girls, with Jimmy, standing on a little bridge a bit like the one on the willow pattern plate – very pretty. There were life-size Chinese models in groups creating different tableaux.

In the evening, back on board ship, the order in which we would be leaving the ship for the airport was announced. As we were not leaving until the next afternoon, we had another half day on board, which gave us the chance to say our goodbyes to friends we had made on our journey. The final evening was the captain's dinner. I remember we had lobster; it was the first time I had tasted it and I have loved it ever since. We all wore party hats, and there was a real party spirit. For dessert, the lights were dimmed and all the waiters came out in single file, weaving in and out of the tables. They held trays aloft with an ice cream confection on each tray. There were sparklers stuck into the desserts, which had been lit. Everyone was clapping and cheering, until a spark ignited a hat on one of the ladies' heads. For a few seconds there were screams, but it was extinguished almost immediately – then everyone cheered and laughed. It was unforgettable!

All too soon we were being loaded on to our buses, after swapping addresses and promising to keep in touch. Jimmy was very sad when it came to saying goodbye, and became quite emotional. I think he had a soft spot for Nicola, and gave her a couple of little gifts to remember him by. But we didn't need presents to remember our trip. He gave us his address in Singapore, but we did not know whether we would hear from him ever again. We gave him my aunt's address to keep him happy, but we really hadn't got a clue where we would be living or even what the future had in store for us. But, as Scarlett O'Hara said, 'Tomorrow is another day.'

We boarded our plane, excited to be going home, but for Bill and me there was also a little apprehension. It was yet another

Diamonds in the Coal Dust

beginning, another start from scratch, but we had done it before and we would do it again. We stopped in Bahrain and got off the plane for a drink and a leg stretch in the airport. That leg stretch lasted for eight hours, as the plane developed a fault that couldn't be fixed. I don't know whether a mechanic was flown out to fix it or if that a replacement part had to be sent for. We had to make the best of it until it was fixed. We were given a meal and were made comfortable, and the time passed quite quickly really.

On arrival at Gatwick, after collecting our luggage, Bill went to organise the rental of a car. We had decided that he would drive us up to Yorkshire, rather than have us cope with the stress of a long train journey. It felt so good to be back in England, but there was also a little sadness, too. Had we failed? Had we done the right thing? Who knew; time would tell. One thing was for sure, I was looking forward to seeing my son again. It was mid-afternoon, so we would be home before nightfall. The girls nodded off on the journey back home – it had been a tiring time for us all, and it would be a while before we got back to normal.

Chapter Five

We arrived at my aunt's house around teatime. It was good to see her again; she didn't look much different. She couldn't believe how much the girls had grown up, but she was so pleased to see us. I think she had thought she would never see us again.

We were all going to squeeze in with her for the moment, until we decided what we would do; things have a way of sorting themselves out. Bill did his usual vanishing trick, and went to the club where he knew his father would be. I put the girls to bed and Aunty and I caught up with the local news. However, when Bill came home around 11 p.m. he had some great news for us. The local council had offered us – through Bill's father – a council house in the same village as Bill's mum and dad, how lucky was that?

This was unbelievable news, although Bill's father said that the house in question was in a bit of a state, as it had been used by several tenants as a transit house while their own homes were being modernised.

Bill's father arranged to go with Bill the next morning to take the hire car back, and then take us to see the house.

He was right, it was in a state, but there was nothing that paint and wallpaper wouldn't fix. It had already been modernised and had three bedrooms, a nice front room and quite a large living kitchen. We went to the council offices and told them that we would have the house, and they told us that there would be a grant to help towards the complete decoration of the house. We actually felt excited, especially as the next port of call was to go and see Martin. That's when things started to unravel. We found out that Martin had not returned to school after all, as we had hoped, but had started work as an apprentice electrician with a local company. I wasn't very happy – in fact, I was more than a

Diamonds in the Coal Dust

little disappointed; Bill was not too happy, either. Apparently, the school had had a fire and some school records had been destroyed. But whatever the ins and outs of it were, we were faced with the fact that Martin had come home on his own, and had got himself a job. He said that he did not want to go back to school anyway. He seemed to like the idea of an apprenticeship, and if he came away with a trade at the end of it, perhaps it wasn't too big a disaster.

Having got the housing problem sorted, Bill paid a visit to his old workplace, to see whether there was any chance of him getting his old job back. His old manager offered him a place and said that he could start the following Monday. I went to the high school which was just round the corner from our house and enrolled Nicola. I had a bus ride to my aunt's village, to visit the junior school which Ann had attended before we went to Australia. She was given a place there to begin the same day as Nicola. It meant that Ann had a bus ride to school, but I put her on the bus at my end and my aunt met her off the bus and saw that she got to school. The return journey was a reversal of the morning trip. It was obvious that we were going to need some form of transport, as Bill would be working shifts, and also we had quite a lot of running about to do, not least for wallpaper and paint. Martin said that he would stay with his grandma for the time being, until we got the house up and running. There was also the small matter of furniture – at the very least, the basics.

Bill managed to pick up an old banger in the village; it was not pretty, but it would get us from A to B until we could afford something better.

We got stuck into the decorating and it was surprising how quickly we got the house into a half-decent state. Bill working the night shift meant that he could be around for most of the day for the decorating.

It was almost as though we had never been away: the girls were back in school, Bill was at the pit, and I was putting all my energies into getting the house squared up as quickly as possible. I notified the haulage company of our address – hopefully we would have more luck in getting our packing case in reasonable time than when we had sent it the other way! It was obvious as well that I was going to have to get a job, at least until we got onto our feet again.

I applied for three jobs and finished up being offered all three. Those were the days! One was at a jeweller's, one at the university and one at the gas board. The hours and conditions at the gas board seemed the best deal, so that was the one I went for. The position was in the cash office, and I travelled by train. I was there for two weeks, but I hated it. The environment was very unfriendly, nobody spoke, and even though I was new to the job, nobody seemed to want to help me out with advice. However, I could not afford not to work, so I immediately looked around for something else. Several of the ladies in the village worked at the local brewery; a bus picked them up in the village, and they all seemed a happy bunch. I applied for a job there and was given a place in the bottling stores. I will never forget my first day there – the noise was horrendous and the smell was something else. Some days I would be on the washer where the bottles came down a conveyor belt, all rattling and jostling. We had to swing them up, six at a time if they were half-pints and four at a time if they were pints. They had to be slotted into the washer non-stop, as the belt was going all the time and you couldn't afford to get a pile-up at the other end. Some days I would be putting the full bottles into wooden crates. It was hectic, and I had muscles like Popeye, but we did manage to have fun at the same time.

Bill was not happy that Martin had still not signed the papers for his apprenticeship, and suggested that he might be better doing an apprenticeship with the NCB. Their training was second to none – or so Bill said. They would pay for Martin to go to technical college, and he would be qualified at the end of four years.

So Bill went to see the manager at the pit, who suggested that Martin go and have a talk with the training officer, to see if Martin would be suited to the task at the pit. When he went for his interview he actually met up with a couple of his pre-Australia school friends, who would be on the same course as him. The only thing putting Martin off was the idea of going down the pit. He thought that it was not for him, but to his credit, he made his mind up that he would do his apprenticeship and get his papers.

Diamonds in the Coal Dust

We had been home a year when I had the chance of a job at the local factory in the management accounts department. Off I went to another new job. The girls in the office were great and my superior was a lovely man. It was a bacon factory and we got a staff discount on any meat products which we purchased.

The next two years flew by. Martin was going out with a lovely girl, Nicola had left school and Ann had started attending the high school. Nicola began work at Lewis's as a junior, training to be a manager, but just as I hadn't liked it at Lewis's all those years ago, neither did Nicola. She applied to join the police force and did well in the entrance exam, but they told her she was one and a half inches too short. As she was still young – she was seventeen years old – they suggested that she should apply again in a couple of years. She thought that if she took a more physical job, she would grow more quickly, so she got a job in the bacon factory. I can't say that I was pleased about it, but it was a means to an end.

After we returned from Australia, we were once more in close contact with the friends who had introduced us to Chris and Mona. We all had many a laugh at the antics of their old neighbours; we filled them in with information on their new life in Australia. Flo, my old friend from Avon, was still working, as her husband Tom, who had suffered from bronchitis for years, had now been diagnosed with emphysema, and was not well at all. They had moved into a bungalow, as Tom could no longer cope with the stairs. Flo and I had many a laugh as we recalled the days out we used to have with my girls when they were young. We would go on the train to Scarborough and stuff ourselves with ice cream and waffles piled high with cream. We would have the obligatory fish and chip lunch, and the kids would probably finish off with candyfloss. Where did we put it all? On the way to the railway station, the girls would call in at the toy shop, a veritable Aladdin's cave. After one of our day trips out, the girls had chosen, of all things, horrendous black wigs, like Indian squaws; they couldn't be persuaded to change their minds, and even wore them all the way home. We still laugh about those wigs to this day.

I corresponded with Monica and George for some months after we returned home, as promised. In one of her earlier letters,

103

she told me that Jan – her daughter – had met and married an Australian man. Monica was very pleased about it. A later letter informed me that their weatherboard house had burned down, and they had been re-housed by a charity organisation in Cessnock. I wrote back to their box number, to try to find out more news, and she replied that they were hoping to move into a mobile home in the garden of the property where Jan and her new husband lived. That was the last I ever heard of them – subsequent letters from me were returned with the note that the people in question were no longer the users of that box number. I even wrote to the local newspaper with a plea for information, but it did not bring any response. I wish I could have found out what happened to them, but they will be remembered by us all.

We had applied to the council for a house transfer, as the house we lived in was next door but one to a shop. Bill worked the night shift, and he was not happy to be woken on a regular basis by the delivery trucks. It was almost impossible for him to sleep, and, when Bill did not get his sleep, he was like a bear with a sore head. So we were hoping for an exchange to a quieter location.

I had begun driving lessons, along with two more girls in the office. One of the girls was Bill's cousin, whom I got on really well with. I hated learning to drive, but it did help that there were three of us, and we encouraged each other. Martin had passed his test some months earlier, and was now the proud owner of his own car. I refused to go for driving practice with Bill, as we always ended up having words and he would manage to shatter the little bit of confidence that I had. We were all three girls learning to drive with the same instructor, and the other two would return from their lesson saying things like, 'Oh, I am doing OK – he says that I am almost ready for my test.' I would return from my lesson thinking, 'What the hell am I doing?' and wishing that there would be ten feet of snow when my next lesson was due. However, in November, after three months of lessons, my instructor uttered the dreaded words: 'You should put in for your test.' My test was booked for 7 November, and the instructor would take me round the same route that he assured me I would be going on my test. However, on the day, it was sleeting and the

Diamonds in the Coal Dust

test centre I was to go to had had its schedule hit by the influenza bug. There was a shortage of examiners, so they had to draft examiners in from another area. The one that I got was one of these, and consequently he took me on a totally different route from the one I was used to. It didn't take much to confuse me, and I felt like saying to him that we were going the wrong way, but he didn't look like he had much of a sense of humour, so I didn't say anything. When it came to reversing round a corner, he took me to one with a wide sweep rather than the tight little corner that my instructor had taken me to. However, the test itself went quite quickly and in no time at all I found myself back at the test centre. I think it went quickly because I was concentrating so hard. The examiner asked me to switch off the engine. I was shaking so much that I could barely move. When he said to me, 'I am pleased to tell you that you have passed', I couldn't even answer him – I just sat there in shock with the pass certificate in my hand. The examiner left, and the driving instructor came to the car. 'There,' he said. 'That wasn't so bad, was it?' I just nodded, my teeth chattering. The instructor drove the car home, and I said to him, 'If I hadn't passed, I wouldn't have taken it again.' 'Oh, but you would,' he said.

When I arrived home, Bill was still in bed after his night shift. I put my pass certificate on top of the TV where it couldn't be missed. My neck was stiff from tension, but I began to feel rather proud, even though I thought I was very lucky to have passed first time. Bill's car was sitting outside the house, so I took the keys, went outside and started it up. Bill's mum and dad lived round the corner, on the other side of the green, and I set off very slowly, moved up one side of the green, and was feeling very pleased with myself... when the car stopped. I tried to start it up again, but it refused to go. I went from hot to cold and back to hot again. I ran down to my father-in-law's house; he was in, fortunately. I told him what had happened and he looked at me as though I was demented, which I was, almost. 'What were you doing driving the car in the first place?' he asked me. I told him that I had just passed my test and had wanted a little practice on my own before Bill got up. There was no 'well done' – he just said, 'Keys.' I put them in his hand and we set off towards the abandoned car. He put the keys in the ignition and asked me, 'Didn't you have the choke out?' 'What's the choke?' I asked him – I didn't know anything about a choke. He pulled the choke out, turned the key and hey presto it started; thank goodness for that. He drove the car as far as his house, where I got in and drove it home – where it stayed until Bill got up. I learned a valuable lesson that day: just because you have a pass certificate doesn't mean you have suddenly become a driver. My learning had just begun.

I had arranged to meet my friends from work at the nearby pub at lunchtime, to either congratulate or commiserate with me. I left Bill still in bed, and walked to the pub. My mates were all very pleased for me, and the other two learners were eager to hear if the test was as bad as everyone said. I had to say that for me it was. When I arrived home one and a half hours later, Bill was up but hadn't noticed my certificate. When I showed it to him, his comment was, 'How much did that cost you?' Oh well – the kids would be pleased. I knew that Bill's dad would tell him about my episode with the car, so I told him myself. 'What would have happened if I had wanted the car?' he asked me. 'It was only round the corner,' I told him. So, battle lines were drawn. If I wanted the car, I would probably have to give a month's notice. It took a long time for me to get across to Bill that I had a right to the car as well, especially when the girls needed taking anywhere.

My aunt, who had suffered from arthritis for years, was getting more infirm, and was finding it increasingly difficult to get up and down the stairs. We applied for her to have a bungalow in the village where she lived, and, after a few months of waiting, she was offered one. It had just one bedroom, but it was big enough for her, and more importantly, it had a bathroom. So there was no more going across the yard to the toilet. There was also a community centre quite near, so if she wanted, she could go and have a game of bingo or just have a natter with the other elderly ladies. Martin and I did the moving for her; it meant getting rid of a lot of things that she had hung on to for donkey's years. It was a bit sad, but we knew that she would be so much more comfortable in her new little pad. She settled in quite nicely, and she hadn't been there very long when the council contacted her to say

My first driving lesson, 1938

On holiday in Morecambe with my uncle and aunt, 1945

Bill amd I on our wedding day, 1956

Me aged sixteen, 1954

Martin and Nicola, 1962

Kids at a street party, 1962
Nicola (at the front, curly hair) and Martin (at the back, striped top)

Ann and Nicola with Star, Australia, 1972

Thelma, myself and Vida having 'fun' in the vineyards, 1972

Bill and I on our silver wedding anniversary, 1981

My four beautiful granddaughters, 2003

Ann and I with Bill in Spain, three months before he passed away, 2004

Me and my lovely children at Bill's memorial service, 2004

Diamonds in the Coal Dust

that her old house was to be compulsorily purchased, as the whole row of cottages was being demolished. They made her a cash offer, which she accepted. It wasn't a fortune, but it was more than she had ever had before. I would have liked her to have done something with it that she really wanted to do – perhaps to go and see her cousin in Canada – but she wasn't interested.

Martin worked at the pit in the same village as my aunt lived, as did Bill, but Martin spent a lot of time there, as many of his friends lived in the same village. He was very good to my aunt; the girls called her Grandma, but Martin always called her Edie B. He was very caring towards her, and the odd Saturday night when he had been out late, he would stay the night, sleeping on her settee.

Since I had passed my test, it was easier, as I could get from our village to my aunt's without having to wait for a bus. One day, not too long after I had passed my test, I was taking Nicola and Ann to see their grandma. It began to snow heavily, and soon I couldn't see through the windscreen. I didn't know where the wipers were, and I was shouting to the girls, 'Can you see anything that says "wipers"?' In the end, I had to pull off the road and try every switch until I found the right one. Oh, the joys of driving. But it did make life easier, because if we wanted to go anywhere and Bill didn't – which was quite often – I would say, 'Come on then, I'll drive.' Somehow the balance of power had shifted only very slightly, but it was a start. I never drove with Bill as a passenger; he was still telling me how to drive ten years after I had passed my test. If we went anywhere together and we came to a road junction, I would look left for him to see if there was anything coming, but I would get his elbow in my throat and a shout of 'I'm driving'.

Meanwhile, Martin had ended his relationship with his girlfriend and was a free agent again, and Nicola had already had one or two forays into the world of 'courting'.

We were offered another house on the next estate. When we went to look at it, it didn't look much different to our present one, but at least we would be away from the shop. We were on the move again, but not too far this time and Bill decided that we didn't need a removal van. I was quite adept at holding one end of a wardrobe – usually the heavy end, I think – while Bill held on to the other. It's unbelievable how much stuff you can transport on a roof rack.

We had hardly moved into our new home when Nicola started to bring a new boyfriend home, very often. She seemed really enamoured with him. I admit he was a bit of a smooth talker, but what can you do as a parent, except keep watch from the sidelines? We didn't know of him or his family, as they were not local to the area. He was apparently a part-time student while working at a paint factory. Quite quickly things became serious. I went to his parents' house for a discussion, but it was a waste of time; the atmosphere was quite surreal, and I came away wondering what the hell I had gone for. However, despite everything, Nicola and he decided that they would get married, and live with us until they got a place of their own. The wedding itself was weird – actually, that is an understatement – and I felt very uneasy. Perhaps we should have said that they couldn't get married, but I remembered when Bill and I were to be married, Bill's mother said that she wouldn't give her permission, so Bill said that we would get married anyway. So there we were – our pretty, bubbly daughter married. Almost at once, things began to go pear-shaped; the new husband left his job and was out of work. This caused some friction, as at our house we were used to working for a living. I got him a job in the lab at the bacon factory, but I don't think he made much of an impression there. I think he was acting like a scientist but working like a plonker. Living under our roof, we were privy to their arguments, of which there were plenty, but eventually they were offered a flat. It was not very posh, but it was a place of their own. We helped to get it kitted out as much as we could, but we were only just getting on our feet again ourselves. We were also having problems with Ann, who had suffered a recurrence of the tummy troubles that she had experienced where she was younger. Things became so bad that the pain made her vomit. We took her to different doctors and she had many tests, but nothing was conclusive. I enjoyed my work, but it didn't help that Nicola and her husband both worked there. I felt as though I saw and heard too much.

Martin, by this time, had completed his apprenticeship, and

Diamonds in the Coal Dust

told his father that pit life was not for him; he was looking for something else. He was still at the pit, and we knew that he would not leave until he got something else. Bill was not too happy, but when Martin said that he did not want to spend the rest of his life working down a black hole, coughing his lungs up with the coal dust, it was hard to argue with him.

He started a correspondence course to train to be a salesman and seemed to be really interested in it – he certainly took it seriously. I was really annoyed with Nicola's husband, who began quizzing Martin about the course and making derogatory remarks about it. How dare he! He would say to Martin, 'What makes you think you could get a job in selling? Come on, try to sell me something and convince me that I should buy it.' I was pleased when Martin answered, 'I don't have to convince you of anything.' Well done, Martin. Our son-in-law wanted to buy a motorbike, as they didn't have any transport and it was difficult for them to get around. The trouble was that he couldn't get finance for it, so Bill agreed to go as guarantor for him. We had a small touring caravan and, when we arranged to go down to Devon on holiday, Nicola and her husband came as well. Ann was travelling with us and we had Nicola's tent and their luggage in the caravan. Ann's friend also came along, so we were quite well piled up. We had a lovely holiday; in fact, I think everybody enjoyed it.

When we arrived home, we found Martin had managed to get an interview with a top biscuit firm as a trainee rep. I was very proud of him. He was enjoying his life – a group of them would go off to the south of France, staying in two caravans. One year, they went to Monte Carlo, as one of their old school mates was working there as a chef. They also paid a visit to the casino – nothing too flamboyant, just a little flutter. They were a decent bunch of lads. I just wish that Bill had got closer to him, but they didn't seem to have a lot in common. Martin was still totally committed to Leeds United, and Bill's great love was still fishing.

Martin drifted in and out of relationships, and was quite happy with things the way they were. Nicola and her husband stuttered along as best they could. We thought that she deserved better, but that was for her to find out. He was full of highfalutin ideas, but with no substance to back them up; we thought that he was totally irresponsible.

One night, we got an urgent phone call. It was our son-in-law, telling us that there had been an accident. Nicola had put her arm through a glass door and had severed an artery, and they were on their way to hospital. We jumped in the car, and dashed there, too. She was in the emergency department, but the doctor came out and told us that she was being transferred to a hospital which specialised in microsurgery. They told us that she would be going under a police escort as she had lost so much blood and it was quite serious. She looked so pale and tiny lying there, I could have killed her husband, even though I didn't know what had happened. We followed the ambulance but we couldn't keep up with it, as it had the siren going and the flashers on. We were very worried. When we arrived at the hospital, they had already taken Nicola into surgery. Bill rounded on his son-in-law, demanding to know what had happened. His explanation was that they had been having a few words (no surprise there), he had gone into the kitchen, and Nicola followed, but he said that he hadn't known that she was behind him and let the kitchen door swing to. Nicola had put out her hand to stop it, and her hand went straight through it. We rang Martin and Ann to let them know what had happened, as we had rushed out of the house without leaving a note. The doctor said that it would be some time before they could tell us anything, so we decided to go back to the flat to clean it up.

When we got to the flat, I couldn't believe my eyes – it was like a slaughterhouse; there was blood everywhere. It was up the walls, on the ceiling – it looked like she had been running through the house while it was spurting out. I suppose she had been panicking. We set to cleaning it up as best we could – at least it would keep our minds off our Nicola. After we had done a half-decent job, we called to see that Ann was OK, and then went back to the hospital.

Nicola's husband was sitting in the waiting room, so we joined him. After goodness knows how long, the doctor came out and said that it was finished. They had repaired the tendon and artery, but they wouldn't know the outcome for some time – that is to say, they didn't know how much movement she would regain. The damage was in the bend of her elbow, and had been done not when she put her arm through but when she pulled it back out. She had, as I said, lost a lot of blood and had needed a transfusion. The doctor told us she would not be awake until morning, and suggested that we go home and come back again tomorrow. We took her husband home but didn't have much to say to him. The next morning when we arrived at the hospital, Nicola was awake but very pale. Her arm was suspended in a sling and completely swathed in bandages. She came home after five days but obviously wasn't able to do anything, and we made sure that she didn't. They told her at the hospital that she had been very lucky; she had the use back in her fingers but they said that she probably would always have a slight weakness in that arm.

After a few weeks, she went back to work. Things weren't much better between her and her husband, but she knew that we were there for her. Nicola had to forget about the police force with her weak arm, but she did not fancy staying at the bacon factory for the rest of her working life.

We were on the move again, or hoping to be. The parking where we lived was a nightmare, and, now that Martin had a car, it was nigh on impossible to park. Ideally, we would have liked to move to a semi.

At Christmas, our office workers would always to go a French restaurant in the village. It was very popular and had to be booked weeks in advance. This time, I chose lobster for my main course; it was delicious and of course we had a few glasses of vino. We were all ladies except for Peter, my boss, and he was usually in charge of paying the bill, after we had worked out how much we individually owed. As the night drew to a close, one by one we said our goodbyes, and went home. When there were just two left, Peter realised that we had all gone off without leaving our money. I think Peter was washing up until the following Christmas.

Nicola had seen an advertisement for a shorthand and typing course, starting in January. It was a very intensive course, to last twenty weeks. The problem was that it was being held in a town twenty miles from where we lived. Nicola had no way of getting there by herself, so she asked me if I fancied going. I thought about it for about thirty seconds, and then said that I would. It was very sad leaving my friends in the office, especially as they had supported me through thick and thin, but we would be keeping in touch.

The first week we were due to start college, the weather was atrocious. It snowed non-stop the night before we began, the motorway was closed and we were late getting there. Not a good start! Everyone was seated by the time we got in; almost all the other students lived locally, so they had no trouble with the journey. The only two seats available were under the nose of the tutor. Great!

Up to lunchtime we had shorthand, then in the afternoon we had typing. It was good fun, if a little intense. It began snowing again in the late afternoon, so it was decided that we should leave for home. For the following two weeks, it didn't improve much, and as I did not enjoy driving in bad weather, it took the fun out of it a bit. Most of the class got on really well together and Nicola and I were called 'the two Ronnies', as the rest of the class looked to us for amusement and to lighten the atmosphere. On Fridays we got into the habit of going to a Chinese restaurant for lunch. We all always had a curry, and when we ordered the meal, we always ordered six glasses of water, one for each of us. For some reason they never brought the water, so we would catch a waitress' eye and ask for six glasses of water. Then, when the meal was brought we would ask them again. We would of course usually end up with eighteen glasses – it was a bit of a standing joke with us.

It took three weeks for the weather to become less severe, and as the relationship between Nicola and her husband did not improve, she decided to come back home. Her husband was still out of work, with seemingly no inclination to do anything about it.

Our time at college passed very quickly and then it was just a matter of waiting for the results. I wasn't too bothered, as I felt that I could get a little job anywhere, but Nicola was hoping for grander things. Ann was still having problems with her stomach

Diamonds in the Coal Dust

and we were still seeking an explanation for the attacks.

Bill began to receive letters about the payments, or lack of payments, for the motorbike which he had stood as guarantor for. Nicola's husband had obviously not been keeping up with the payments and Bill was liable. Bill went to the flat and brought the bike back with him; he reckoned that if he was going to pay for the bike, then he might as well have ownership of it. He also managed to get his son-in-law a job at the pit. To the lad's credit, he did give it a try, but not for very long. He eventually gave the flat up and moved back in with his parents.

Our exam results came in, and they were OK for me but brilliant for Nicola. She immediately began the search for a clerical job, while I got myself a job at the local school as a cleaner. It suited me at the time, as it gave me time to keep an eye on my aunt. I had acquired a little old banger, which was very useful. My job was on a split-shift basis – I went in at 6.30 a.m. until 8.30 a.m., and then 3.45 p.m. until 6 p.m. It was a bit restrictive but it worked out OK.

Nicola was offered a job in Leeds with a house-building firm as a junior typist. I was so proud of her, and it was the best thing that could have happened. She had applied to get a divorce, and she was starting to get her life back on track. Just at that time, we were offered another house, in a small hamlet about four miles outside our village. We went to have a look at it and were impressed. There were six houses in all: two farmhouses, two bungalows and two farms. It was very quiet with open fields to the back and front of the property, which was semi-detached. Beautiful! There was one snag – the previous tenants had done a runner, and had left most of their stuff in the house. Just as we were getting our heads round the idea that we had the chance of another new start, Ann became very ill again. I was at work when Bill came to take me home as Ann was going to have to go to hospital again. When I arrived back home, Ann was on the floor vomiting with pain. In she went to hospital again for tests. All this, and we had to make a decision about the house. Bill contacted the council, and they agreed to give us two weeks' grace in order to get the new house cleared of all the paraphernalia that had been left in it. Meanwhile, in spite of all the tests, once more nothing conclusive was found to be wrong with Ann. It seems to me that if a female has any sort of problem, the medical profession tends to put it down to age, regardless of what that age actually is.

After three weeks of concerted effort from all of us, we moved house. It was a different world. Looking out of the bedroom window one early morning, I saw a fox in the field; the next morning, out of the same window, I saw a deer... how lovely was that?

Martin was offered his own sales territory; the only thing was that it was in the north-east, which meant that ideally he would have to live in that area. He looked for and found a property in Whitley Bay, which was ideal for his travels, but meant another of my birds would be flying the nest. Bill and I helped him to move into his new place; it was very nice and did have a sea view when he bought it, but shortly afterwards some new apartments were built, and the view disappeared – but it was still very pleasant. He usually came back to Yorkshire at the weekend to go out with his mates, and usually stayed at my aunt's on Saturday nights. However, that changed when he found a girlfriend who lived up in the north-east, although we saw them both on a regular basis.

There had been rumours for some time that Bill's pit was to close down, and as there had been a big coal development in the area, miners were offered the chance of a transfer to one of the more modern pits. Bill chose one of the more established pits, and looked forward to the move. For some time there had been little or no bonus at his old pit, as it was very old, with old workings.

Nicola and I usually managed to have a laugh together, and we both liked a challenge, so when I saw an advert in the paper for film extras, we were up for it. The film was called *Chariots of Fire*, and extras were needed for a scene which was to be shot in York. We were to send brief details about ourselves and a photo to an address in Leeds. I arranged to meet Nicola in her lunch hour to have our photos taken in one of those little booths. I had mine done, but then some of Nicola's coins would not work in the machine. No problem, she said, she would have it done after work... except that she didn't. I, in the meantime, had posted my photo and details – not that I expected to hear anything more. A week or so later, we were having tea when the phone rang. It was the casting company, asking whether I would be available for a costume fitting the next day. I thought that Nicola had arranged to have one of her friends ring me as a joke, but she assured me that she hadn't had anything to do with it. The kids thought it was hilarious, but the next morning, as I was off to be given the once-over, I could see stardom beckoning. The hall where I had been told to go was huge and heaving with people. Ladies were queuing up to be fitted with gowns and hats suited to the early 1900s, while in another queue the gentlemen were assembled, trying on striped blazers and straw boaters. There were also little booths where younger men were having their hair cut to conform to the hairstyles of the period. After I was allocated a gown (which bore the name of Thora Hird) and a cloche hat, my name was written on a card which was pinned to the garment. We were then told that a bus would pick us up the next morning; we had to be dressed in our allocated costumes before we got on the bus. We were told to expect to be away for most of the day. It was all so exciting.

The next morning, I was there bright and early, and met up with a couple of ladies whom I had spoken to the day before. On the bus, we were told that we were going to York railway station for the filming, and that instructions would be relayed to us as and when we needed them. One platform of the station had been closed for filming, and a huge steam train was sitting on the platform. There was a big chuck wagon outside where we could get plenty of refreshments when we felt the need. It was quite a long day, as the scene involved Ben Kingsley and some of the other stars arriving back from the Olympics, and the scene had to be shot and re-shot before it was acceptable – they had the patience of Job. We hung around all day and were only called in the last thirty minutes or so. But I wouldn't have missed it for the world, and we were paid £25. Whenever *Chariots of Fire* is on TV, I always think of that day, and, because I knew where I was standing on the set, I can just about pick out the top of my hat as I move across the screen. But sadly, that was my only claim to fame, and I wasn't even mentioned in the credits.

Nicola was learning to drive, and she had obtained her divorce from her husband, so she was getting her life back on track. Bill loved his new place of work; his wages were twice as much as he had been getting at the old pit, as the bonus was extremely good. It was a record-breaking pit, churning out some of the highest yields in Europe, and they regularly exceeded their targets. Bill had carried his holidays over when he moved to the new place, and we were considering going back to Australia for a holiday. We would probably go for a month, as I well remembered the jet lag I suffered when I went the first time. I wrote a letter to Monica and George, telling them that we were going and would like to look them up, but never received a reply. We were planning to stay with Mona and Chris, who by now lived in a housing association place on the outskirts of Wollongong. Martin said that he would keep an eye on my aunt, who was becoming more frail and didn't venture far on her own. Ann had left school and was working at the chemist's in the village, and could get the bus at the end of our lane. A few days before we were due to fly out, Bill went down with 'flu. It was very rare for Bill to be ill, apart from the problem with his back. Up until the last minute, we weren't sure whether we would be going; however, he said that he felt much better, and the sunshine would do him good. Martin and his friend drove us to the airport, and Bill slept for most of the way to Gatwick.

I must say that the flight was much more comfortable than when we had gone with the kids, and there were some vacant seats so we could stretch out as well. Bill fell asleep almost as soon as we took off, and actually slept through a meal, which he was very perturbed about afterwards. Sleep was probably the best thing for him though, as he was still not 100 per cent fit. I didn't sleep as I was too afraid of missing something. We touched down in Bombay but it was bucketing it down, as it was the monsoon season, so we didn't get off the plane.

When we arrived in Sydney, Chris was waiting for us, and when we stepped out of the airport it was as if we had never been away. The smells and the warmth felt so familiar. We arrived at Chris's house in just over an hour, and it was nice to meet up with Mona

Diamonds in the Coal Dust

again. We had a real old natter over a cup of tea; she wanted to know all about her neighbours, Flo and Tom, and about the kids. They had arranged for us to go out with them that evening to the Yacht Club. Apparently they went somewhere different nearly every night. A couple of nights a week they played bingo; they also played indoor bowls and a game called euchre, which I had never heard of. But Mona said that she would give it all up if she could go back home tomorrow. I couldn't keep my eyes open that first night, but the next morning I was raring to go. I went for a walk with Mona for a look round the area, while Chris and Bill got under the bonnet of Chris's car to try to sort out a problem that he had. It looked to me like it wanted mending with a new one. After a couple of days of unwinding, we decided to hire a car and drive up to Cessnock to look up some of our friends. It felt good to be flying up the Pacific Highway again. We came into Cessnock from the top end so that we could drive past our old house. We were staggered when we arrived there – the house was gone. The tall trees, the fence, the magnolia and the jacarandas were still there, but, where the house had been, the land had gone back to nature – overgrown and wild. I don't know why we felt sad, but we did.

We made our way down into Vincent Street, which hadn't changed. We actually booked into the same hotel that we had stayed in all those years ago – ten years, to be exact. The owners were new; apparently the original owners had retired, and were now on a world tour. We parked the car and walked down the wide street. The Carousel Bar was still there, and the Big W store and Cec Ainstey's, the shop which sold school uniforms and so on. Nothing much had changed in Vincent Street. We returned to the hotel and changed for our evening meal. Afterwards, we decided to go to the club that Bill used to frequent with his mates.

As we walked through the doors, Bill spotted one of his old drinking buddies, little Mickey Manderson, sitting alone at a table. Bill pulled me back and said, 'Just walk past and see if he recognises us.' I walked past him and Bill followed slowly. Mickey looked up and frowned, and then the realisation hit him. He jumped up and hugged Bill and started crying; it was very emotional. 'Jeez,' he said, 'I can't believe it, are you back for good?' Bill explained that we were just back for a holiday. They talked about the last time they had seen each other, when they had had a boozy send-off for Bill and presented him with a tankard. Mickey couldn't believe that it was ten years ago. It was good to hear them reminiscing. Bill asked about the other mates, and Mickey said that they would be in the following night. We had a couple of drinks with him and then went back to our hotel.

The next morning, we set off to try to find out what had happened to Monica and George. Nobody we asked seemed to know anything about them. We went to the site of their old house, but, like ours, you couldn't even tell that a house had been there. We went and looked on the electoral roll, and were surprised to find that there was no mention of them. I was very disappointed. In the afternoon, we went to look up Nicola's friend Jan at her parents' house. Jan's dad, Wick, came to the door and recognised us immediately. 'Jan doesn't live here now that she is married,' he said. 'If you come back this evening, Sandra will take you to see her.' Sandra was Jan's mum, and when we returned later that day, she threw the door open and yelled, 'Jeez, you look younger!' I couldn't say the same for her, but it was nice to hear her say that. We also thought that Wick looked much older, but apparently he had been ill for some time. We had a natter with Sandra and Wick, and Bill had a drink or two before we went in Sandra's car over to the south of Cessnock. The house was an older style, weatherboard property set back from the road. We followed Sandra into the house, and she shouted, 'Jan, I have a surprise for you.' Jan had been in the bath with her toddler son, but came running out, stark naked. She was always a big girl, but now she was even bigger. She didn't bat an eyelid when she saw us, she just shouted, 'Wow, have you brought Nicola with you?' I had to say that there were only the two of us, but of course she wanted to know all about the three of our kids – who, of course, weren't kids any more. She herself had two children, aged three and two, and seemed very happy with her life. It was hard to believe that it was ten years since the girls were riding round on their horses. She actually still had her horse, Bubs, although she was a very old lady by now.

It was strange how the two girls had chosen very different

Diamonds in the Coal Dust

paths in life. Jan was surprised that Nicola had actually been married but was now divorced. They had both come a long way since Jan called Bill 'Billy white legs' and he used to call her 'fat Pat'. We arranged to meet up the following day and continue swapping tales.

The next morning, we went to look up another of Nicola's pals. Kay and Nicola had spent a lot of time together rehearsing for the music and dramatics society. We turned up at Kay's mum's house, but were told that Kay no longer lived there. She was now a nursing sister upstate in a place called Singleton. We took her address and promised to give it to Nicola so that they could get in touch. We later went back to the club to meet up with Jan and her parents but, unfortunately, only Wick turned up – Jan and Sandra had not been able to make it, but at least we had touched base for Nicola's sake.

Of course, we were very disappointed at not being able to track Monica and George down, but we felt that we had done everything possible to find them.

Before we went back to Wollongong, we had to do one more thing, and that was to try one of Newcastle's famous Derby pies. They were out of this world. We ate them hot and, as the Aussies did, we filled the hole in the middle with tomato ketchup. 'Food of the gods.' We then bought a kilo of king prawns, drove out to the vineyards, and sat and shelled the prawns and ate them. We didn't see anybody we knew there, but of course a lot of water had flowed under the bridge since the last time we were there.

We headed back to Wollongong with mixed feelings – we were pleased that we had renewed contact with Nicola's friends, but disappointed at the lack of progress with our own old friends.

The first week of our holiday was over very quickly. We had originally thought that four weeks might be too long, but I didn't think that was going to be the case any more. When we arrived back at Chris and Mona's house, Chris told Bill that his car was playing up again. One thing about Bill was that he did know a bit about cars; he always kept his own vehicle in tip-top condition. He suspected that Chris had been messing about with the engine, but Chris denied it. Mona and I caught a bus into town and had a pleasant half-day pottering about the shops before having a good

Aussie pub lunch. While we were in Australia, St Patrick's Day was celebrated, and when going to one of Chris and Mona's many clubs, we were told to wear something green. It was really good fun, with plenty of Irish music, which Bill loved, and plenty of Guinness flowing, which he loved even more. We had a lovely lunch, which is one thing that the Aussies are good at – their club lunches are great. After that, there was Irish dancing and plenty of laughs and good humour.

We took a trip to see Chris and Mona' daughter and her family. They lived on the other side of Wollongong. They had a wide circle of friends, and one or the other of them was always having a barbecue.

Mona was still very homesick, and told me that they were planning a holiday back home in the not-too-distant future. Chris, on the other hand, loved the life and threw himself into anything and everything. Two nights a week they would play carpet bowls; it was called the chuck run. They played the game in pairs, Mona with one partner and Chris with another. The prizes were chickens, or 'chucks' as the Aussies called them. So if Mona and her partner won a game, then Chris and his partner won, then there would be a semi-final and a final. It was not unusual for the pair of them to go home with four chickens in one night. Their freezer was full of them – as a result, chicken was the staple diet. Not that I minded, as chicken was my favourite meat. For our last week in Australia we decided to get some sun – Mona liked to keep out of it, as it used to get a bit too hot for her. Each morning, Bill and I would get on a bus at the end of the street, and ride into Wollongong, which only took about ten minutes. We would get off the bus at the top of George Street, and walk gently down the length of the main street. When you got to the end, you were on the beach. We had this to ourselves, and there was a little bar where we could buy burgers. The seagulls would form a circle round us, waiting for titbits, and we would spend the rest of the afternoon stretched out in the sun. Around 4 p.m. we would walk back up the main street, past the shops, call and have a coffee, and then catch the bus back.

I couldn't believe how quickly that month went by, and in no time at all, we were off to the airport to catch our flight home. It

Diamonds in the Coal Dust

was a bit emotional saying goodbye to Chris and Mona, but we knew that it wouldn't be too long before they came for their holiday.

I was looking forward to seeing my kids again, and catching up on all their news. Martin met us at the airport to drive us home. It was lovely to see him. He said that everything had gone well while we were away. The girls were at work, but when they came home and we swapped news, I was surprised at how well they had managed without us. Even the washing was up to date!

Chapter Six

Things settled back into the usual routine quite quickly. I went to see my aunty, and she seemed to have got smaller somehow. She told me that she had been stung on the cheek while she was hanging out her washing, but I had to laugh when she told me that the wasp had stung her once and then came back and stung her again. 'How did you know it was the same one?' I asked her. 'Did it have its name on its back?' She had a laugh at that.

Nicola was doing very well at work, and taking on more and more responsibility. I was glad that we had done the secretarial course; it was the making of Nicola. She had passed her driving test, so we decided to dispose of my old banger, and to get a newer car that we could share. It worked out OK, as Nicola went on the bus to work, and had the car at weekends and at night, while I had it through the day to get to work and to see my aunt.

Martin took my aunt to his place in Whitley Bay for a few days – she thought that was great. He had to carry her up the stairs but once she was up there, everything was on one level. Martin would push her along the seafront in her wheelchair, and she thought it was a great adventure.

Things were rubbing along quite nicely, and we had decided to buy our house. It was in such a lovely location, and there were things that Bill wanted to do to the house to improve it. However, there were murmurings that there was trouble brewing between the NCB and the government. But that year Christmas and New Year were happy family events. On Christmas Eve, Bill went to the pub – no change there. I said to Nicola that I was thinking of going to midnight mass, so Nicola said that she would come, too. Martin and Ann were out with friends, and Nicola went out early, promising to be back in time to go to church. I had prepared the veggies and put the presents out and so on, when around 11 p.m.

Diamonds in the Coal Dust

the phone rang. 'Mum, would you mind if I didn't go with you to church?' It was Nicola, sounding decidedly the worse for wear. Why wasn't I surprised? So at 11.30 p.m. I got the car out and set off down into the village to go by myself. It was so quiet and there wasn't a soul about – I thought that there must have been a cancellation or something. However, I went up to the church door and turned the handle. It gave out the loudest squeak and when I pushed it open, the church was packed to the rafters – everyone kneeling in prayer. I crept in, hot with embarrassment, and slid into a little space on the end of one of the pews. I hadn't realised that it actually began at 11.30 p.m. and not midnight. However, I was glad that I went; there is something so magical about coming out of the church on Christmas Eve.

My aunt stayed over the New Year, and again all the boozers in the house had gone out. Wherever Martin was, and regardless of who he was with, he was always the first to ring home to wish us a happy New Year. My aunt had decided to go to bed as she was falling asleep. I helped her upstairs and into bed, but very soon afterwards I heard a bump. I ran upstairs and found my aunt on the floor; she had bumped her cheek on the corner of the dressing table. I felt awful and blamed myself, but she assured me that she was fine. Not a great start to the New Year, though.

In the spring, the trouble which had been rumbling between the miners and the government exploded into all-out war. The whole of the Yorkshire coalfield was on strike. I was the union rep at school; I didn't want the job but neither did anyone else, so I used to go to the union meetings and try as best I could to represent the women cleaners.

At the same time as the pit strike was beginning, my aunt became quite ill. She didn't seem to want to get out of bed, and didn't want to eat anything. I would go and do my early shift at work, and then go through to get my aunt up, carrying her into the lounge and getting her breakfast, whether she wanted it or not. I would leave her a flask and sandwiches for her lunch, before going back to work for my evening shift. I would then return to give her tea before getting her ready for bed, and tucking her up. After a few days of this, it was too much for her and she didn't get out of bed at all. The doctor came and seemed to think that she might have a tummy bug, but on his third visit he decided that she should go into hospital for some tests. He suspected that she might have had a slight heart attack. He rang for an ambulance and I was to follow in my car. My aunt sent me to the shop for one or two things to take for her. She gave me a list as she always did. I thought that she might be nervous, as she had never been in hospital before, but she took it all in her stride. I packed a bag for her and told her that I would be there as soon as her. When the ambulance man came inside for her, one of them said to her, 'What have you been doing?' She answered, 'I've had a heart attack.' 'Well,' he said, 'you're the liveliest lady I've seen with a heart attack.' He noticed the bottle of Lucozade that I had bought for her. 'What are you doing with that rubbish?' he asked her. 'It does me good,' she told him.

We drove to the hospital, which was about half an hour's drive away. I pulled up at the same time as the ambulance. I think that my aunt had enjoyed the banter with the ambulance men. The staff got to work settling her in; she was in a nice little ward with three more elderly ladies. I left her, to do my afternoon shift, promising her that I would be back to see her that evening. When I returned, later in the day, they had been running some tests on her, and the doctor said they showed that there was some damage to her heart. But she was sitting up in bed, large as life, doing the *Daily Express* crossword, which she had done every day for as long as I could remember.

The other three ladies in her ward did not look very well at all, and always seemed to be asleep whenever I went. My aunt, however, chatted away, asking about the kids. I told her they would be going to see her the next day, which was a Saturday. I took her the daily paper each afternoon, and she always read it avidly. She asked about the miners' strike. 'Do you think it will last long?' she said. We assured her that it would probably be all over quite soon. She was really pleased to see the children; Nicola and Martin went on Saturday, and Ann went with me on the Sunday. She told me that she hadn't eaten anything when I went to see her on Sunday night, as she hadn't fancied anything. I promised to take her a piece of chicken the next afternoon, and she seemed pleased about that. At lunchtime on Monday, I

Diamonds in the Coal Dust

cooked a chicken breast and wrapped it in foil, so that when I arrived at the hospital it was still warm. My aunt was not sitting up when I got there – she told me that she felt tired. She didn't even have her glasses on, which was very unusual for her. She said that her eyes hurt. I thought that she didn't look well. I had a word with the nurse, and she told me that they had done more tests, and things were OK. When I left my aunt, I told her not to forget to eat her chicken, and she promised that she would. In the evening, Bill went with me to see her. She had not touched her chicken, and told me to take it home for Bill. She didn't even seem to want to talk, she just looked old. When we were leaving, I turned at the end of the ward to wave to her, as I always did, but she didn't even notice. I said to Bill, 'She doesn't look well, does she?' Bill agreed with me, but said that she was probably just tired, as they probably didn't get much sleep in those places, with something always going on.

During that night, or to be precise, at 4 a.m., I woke up. I was sweating profusely and felt really ill, as though I had influenza. I staggered to the toilet and had a drink and was just going back into the bedroom when the telephone rang. I knew immediately who it was. A voice at the other end of the phone said, 'I am really sorry, but your aunt has just passed away.'

'Did she ask for me?' I asked her.

'No,' she said, 'she just pressed her buzzer and by the time we had got to her she had collapsed and died.'

I didn't really believe the nurse, as something had alerted me at 4 a.m. and had woken me up. I told her I would go to the hospital the next morning. I went downstairs and made myself a cup of tea. I was in a daze. My aunt was dead. My aunt, who was eighty-six years old. My aunt, who only had to say to my kids, 'I'll look over your head and see your nose,' to bring them into line (until they were old enough to realise just how serious a threat it wasn't). My aunt, who genuinely believed that good people get their reward in heaven, and that God doesn't pay his debts in money. I hope for her sake that she was right. And my aunt, who never said 'I love you' – but I am sure that she did. I cried for her.

She didn't have much of value; most of her possessions went to an auction for charity. She had a cardboard box – about fifteen inches by twelve inches, and twelve inches deep, with a lid on it – in which she kept all the things which were of value to her: old photographs from the turn of the century, ration books and ID cards from the Second World War, letters from her husband during the First World War. That little box was all that was to show for eighty-six years of life, and I kept it and took it with me wherever I went and through all the moves and journeys that I made thereafter. She had always been such a patient lady, and peaceful somehow. She hardly ever swore or raised her voice. She did like to watch wrestling on the television, and when Jackie Pallo or Mick McManus were doing their dirty deeds for the camera, she would yell, 'Ooh, you bugger, and that's swearing.' That was the full extent of her bad language.

There was not much money left over, but I did buy her a headstone for her grave, so that anyone who went to the churchyard would know that my aunty was there.

Chapter Seven

The miners' strike grew ever more ugly, but in our village support for the miners was almost 100 per cent. Local businesses donated food, and the miners' wives were a magnificent support, even setting up their own support group. I went on a picket line in my capacity as union rep. I so admired the miners – it was heart-breaking, seeing how they were being treated. They had to put up with terrible degradation in the name of the government. The police, who had always had the respect of the community pre-strike, lost all of it in the first few weeks by their treatment of the miners, who were, after all, only standing up for their rights. Suddenly they didn't have any rights; good hard-working men, who were no hooligans, were nevertheless being treated as such. I think to this day that the police force is still paying the price for its actions, especially in the villages with such close-knit communities. The power that Maggie Thatcher gave to the police was nothing short of criminal. On one of the picket lines, the men had been loaned a hut as shelter from the elements by one of the local businesses. The police went in and wrecked it, using it as a toilet, and the pickets could do nothing about it.

One year later, nobody watching TV footage of the miners marching behind their own local brass bands, with their banners held aloft and their heads held high, could fail to be moved – at least, nobody who had a heart. Margaret Thatcher didn't win, the miners didn't win; there were only losers. But every single one of those hard-working miners had more integrity in one of their black, broken fingernails than Mark Thatcher had in his whole body.

So, there it was – the miners went back to work, Martin was happy in his job, Nicola was going from strength to strength at work, Ann was enjoying working at the chemist and my aunt had died. Me – I was still a scrubber at the school, but it suited me; no stress, no dramatics, a bit of money in my pocket and in my bank book – plus the hours suited me.

Bill finally came into his own as we were buying the house. We decided that it was time to make a few changes. We had central heating installed, which was an event in itself. It probably took nearly three days to complete and I was fed up of living on a bombsite, as they had taken the fireplace out to put the boiler in. Of course, there were no carpets down and when Bill went to work at lunchtime the workmen had not finished. Nicola was at home that day, so we were instructed to tidy the lounge up after the men had finished. We moved the furniture out, washed the floor and rolled the carpet back down. I had a dresser that had been emptied apart from a couple of commemorative mugs; these were Ovaltine mugs with two lugs on either side for handles. We had a standing joke that the handles looked like Prince Charles's ears. We began to move the dresser slowly into place, but suddenly one of the mugs toppled over and fell to the floor. After the initial horror, we put the dresser in its rightful place and began to pick up the broken pieces of crockery. Scrabbling about on the floor, I shouted, 'I've found one of Charles's ears!' Nicola shouted, 'And I've found the other!' We collapsed into fits of laughter, thinking it was hilarious, but if Bill had been there he would have called us 'a couple of silly b—s'. But we got the job done, and it was no hassle as we had a laugh while we were doing it. By the time Bill came home, the house was presentable. Of course, he didn't say 'well done', but we were happy.

We were thinking of having the kitchen fitted next; after all these years, Bill was becoming house-proud and there was no end to his aspirations. The following Easter, the girls had gone off with individual friends, and Martin had stayed up in Whitley Bay with his girlfriend. I was watching TV and knitting, when suddenly there was an almighty bang and a lump of plaster flew out of the wall and hit me on the back of the head. Bill had started his next project and, once he made his mind up, it was all systems go. I had no chance to cover anything up. I quickly grabbed my best ornaments, threw covers over the suite and he was away. He was knocking a doorway through from the kitchen to the lounge,

Diamonds in the Coal Dust

and the plan was to brick up the existing doorway so that there would be more wall space for the units which he would be installing.

We trawled round all the sales for units, worktops, a double sink, mixer taps and a double built-in oven with ceramic hob and extractor fan. Everything we bought was in the sales. We couldn't believe the bargains that we got, although we did travel some miles to get everything we wanted.

We had a plan drawn up, so that the units we had ordered would fit exactly. Bill wouldn't pay delivery charges, so everything had to be transported on the roof rack. I have lost count of the times I have suffered near-decapitation riding in the car with Bill, my nose pressed up against the window and a worktop or a piece of wood pressing on my jugular vein. I had to beg Bill to slow down, as I could see myself being catapulted through the windscreen if we had to brake suddenly, followed by the timber or formica or whatever I was supporting on my shoulders. All that, after helping to manhandle said items either into the car or on top. Bill would roll up to the car with his overloaded trolley, and there was usually a young man who would say, 'Would you like a hand with that, mate?'

'No thanks,' says Bill. 'I can manage.' Then he would turn to me and say, 'Get 'old, lift your end up a bit.' GRRR! But it was exciting, unpacking all the purchases. But I cast my mind back to our wedding in church, when I looked round and read the Aisle Altar hymn, and then I think somewhere along the line he altered me.

While we were waiting for the kitchen units to arrive, there was plenty of preparation to be done. The wiring for the oven had to be re-sited, as the original cooker was a small freestanding one which stood behind the kitchen door. Martin had turned up to help with the electrics and Bill had gone off to work, leaving strict instructions for Martin to run the electric cable from one side of the kitchen to the other, up in the loft, to come out behind where the new oven was to be housed. Nicola, Ann and I were in the lounge as Martin banged about upstairs. After a while, he shouted, 'Can you have a look and check if you can see the cable yet?'

'No,' we shouted back to him. More banging and then, 'Can you see it yet?' Again, we had to say no. 'But you must be able to, I'm feeding it through.' It was then we noticed that the cable was hanging through a hole in the ceiling of the lounge. Cue fits of laughter from the three of us. We broke the news to Martin, and he quickly pulled it back up again. We knew that Bill would not be amused, so I climbed up the steps, stuffed a piece of paper in the hole and covered it up with a bit of tile cement. You could hardly see it – well, not unless you looked really closely. Funnily enough, a couple of years later Bill spotted the mark on the ceiling. 'What's that?' he asked. I nearly choked on my cornflakes. 'I don't know,' I lied, with my fingers crossed. He didn't pursue it any further. Martin in the meantime measured how far he had to track back with the cable and it duly appeared in exactly the right place. All we had to do now was wait for the units to arrive in stock.

We were notified a couple of weeks later and, as there was a long weekend coming up, Bill was anxious to get his hands on the units so that he would have the whole of that long weekend to work on them. As he had to go to work, Martin was roped in to go and pick the units up on the Friday afternoon. I was to go with him, to show him where the factory was. We were fully equipped with the roof rack, and the seats were reclined in readiness. When Martin saw how many packages there were, he was horrified. The car was loaded to the gunnels and I swear my backside was trailing on the tarmac, the car was so low. We drove home very slowly, with Martin saying repeatedly, 'I hope my boss doesn't see me.' It was a company car and not built to transport an entire kitchen! We made it home safely, though, and Bill came home from work dying to get started, but I persuaded him to wait until morning.

The next morning, Martin was going to watch Leeds United as usual, so it was me and Bill. I was the labourer. I myself was quite excited, as I had never had a new kitchen before. Bill seemed to know what he was doing, and in no time at all had assembled the units ready for putting them in place. The sink unit was the priority, and then he worked his way round from there. I was the tool passer and the tea maker – both very important jobs.

Diamonds in the Coal Dust

It all went very well without Bill losing his temper once, which was very unusual. The oven housing was to be put in place the next day, when Martin would be able to lend a hand.

Sunday morning arrived, and Bill was up bright and early to tackle the last leg of the kitchen units. The oven housing was no problem to install, and they had soon managed to place the double oven in situ. There was just one final piece of the jigsaw, a three-drawer unit to fit by the side of the sink. It was then discovered that the gap left to receive the unit was one inch too narrow. OOPS! Bill didn't stick fast – he told Martin to sit on the floor, with his feet up against the wall, then Bill sat back to back with Martin, with his feet against the drawer unit. 'Right,' he said to Martin, 'when I say push, you push like hell against my back.' Bill pushed with his feet against the unit and it took some persuading but it finally went in, never to come out again. During the operation, Martin and I were trying to stifle our laughter while Bill, as usual, used some very blue language to persuade the drawers into place.

It was quite difficult for Bill to cut a piece out of the worktop for the electric hob to drop into; in fact, Bill said that it was one of the hardest parts of the whole kitchen-building process. But Bill being Bill, he did not stick fast, and it wasn't long before he had cracked it. It all looked gorgeous.

A few years before, we had been on holiday to Spain and Bill had become interested in the work going on at a hotel nearby. A group of workmen were laying beautiful tiles on the floor of a new bar. They made it look so easy, and the effect was stunning. Bill was very impressed, and now decided to do the same in our new kitchen. I wasn't too sure, and wondered whether this time he might have bitten off more than he could chew. But he wasn't phased, and we bought a style of ceramic tile that complemented the units – they were in the sale, of course. It didn't take him much more than a day to lay the lot, as it wasn't too big a kitchen, and the effect was stunning. I could not believe what a marvellous job Bill had done, and without any experience. He said to me, 'Do you think that I could do this for a living?' But I had to tell him that his prospective clients would only employ him if they had earmuffs on and he was wearing a gag over his mouth, so that they could not hear the strong language. But everyone who came to the house was very impressed with the work that Bill had done. I myself was very proud of him.

Nicola had been friendly with a young man for a couple of years, and they were thinking of becoming engaged. Ann was also seeing a chap, but I didn't think that it was going anywhere. Martin was looking for another job within an area more local, and landed a position as area rep for Yorkshire with a firm which sold tinned goods. He sold his place in Whitley Bay and found a very nice semi in Wetherby. His relationship with his girlfriend from the north-east fizzled out and he was a free agent once again. He busied himself with getting his house shipshape; he employed workmen for any job that he could not do himself, unlike his dad.

Ann's boyfriend, Jason, worked for BT, and was a motorbike fanatic (as was Ann herself), and at weekends they would get done up in their leathers and go off for a ride. One year they rode to Italy for the Grand Prix. There was a group of them, and one of his close friends, Jack, had the farm near our house. On Tuesdays, the boys would roar off on their bikes out into the open country for a couple of hours. Ann, together with Jack's wife, who was expecting a baby any time, would get a Chinese takeaway, ready for when the boys came home. The boys had been gone about an hour when Ann received a phone call to say that there had been an accident, and that Jason was in hospital. That was all we knew at that time; it wasn't until the next morning that we knew just how serious it was. They were transferring him to a hospital nearby which specialised in spinal injuries. Apparently, Jason had begun to overtake a vehicle and had been hit by an oncoming car. His spine was damaged, but they wouldn't know the full extent of his injuries immediately.

As Ann did not drive, and Pinderfields was quite a journey, it fell to me to take Ann to see Jason. I would do my morning shift at the school, come home and then take Ann through to the hospital to stay with Jason all day until I picked her up at night. After the first few worrying days, it became obvious that it was a very serious situation. Jason was paralysed from just below the chest.

Diamonds in the Coal Dust

Nicola and Andrew, now her fiancé, were planning their wedding, and we had a letter from Chris and Mona to say that they were coming for a holiday. They were planning to stay with their elder daughter some miles away, but would also be coming to stay with us.

Bill decided on his next project, which was the bathroom. It was quite small and the toilet was in a separate adjoining room, also quite small. The plan was to knock the wall through between the two rooms, making one decent-sized room. He knocked the wall through – no problem, he loved that part – then bricked the door up which had been the access to the toilet. It was unbelievable how much more room there was. The old bathroom suite was to go and a new one to be installed. He installed a shower and put in a sliding door made of plastic which completely enclosed the shower, making it private. The old bath was of the heaviest cast-iron type and would go to the farm, to use for the horses to drink from. Martin had been commandeered to help Bill with the removal of the old bath as it was so heavy. It was a gorgeous summer day, and Nicola and I were sitting outside the front door, telling the tale while the men were working. Suddenly we heard a yell: 'Look out!' The bath had broken free from the rope that was supposed to be holding it, and it hurtled down the stairs, bumping on every step. We leapt out of the way and it flew straight out of the front door. Ann and I were hysterical, and even Martin and Bill had to smile, it was so funny.

As usual, Bill did an excellent job in the bathroom; there was a hell of a mess while it was going on, but it was well worth it.

Chris rang to say that he and Mona were coming up to Yorkshire the next day; we were looking forward to seeing them again. We thought they might feel a little chilly after the heat of Australia, so we made sure that there was a fire up the chimney back. I had cooked a big pan of stew and dumplings to warm them up, too. They couldn't stand it – we had to open the doors, and Chris even got up during the night and opened the bedroom window wide. We had a lovely time with them. We had a day in York and took them to the coast, and spent plenty of time reliving our time in Australia. Mona asked me whether I had any regrets or if there was anything that I particularly missed. I had to say to her that I hadn't really had the time and I didn't see any point in having regrets. Mona still felt homesick, but she did admit that they were so much better off in Australia than at home. We saw them off at the end of their visit; they were going back to their daughter's but we promised that we would see them before they went back.

Bill had leaded the downstairs windows, and it really added character to the house. He kept promising to do the upstairs ones. One afternoon, Nicola and I had our heads together, discussing the forthcoming wedding and having a laugh as usual, when Bill came in, poking about with something. Nicola suggested that we went up to her bedroom to continue our conversation. We were lying on her bed and having a laugh about something or other when suddenly a ladder appeared at the bedroom window. It was Bill, who had suddenly decided to put the leading on the window. We looked at each other, then Nicola calmly stood up, went to the window and pulled the curtains shut. We could hear Bill swearing from where we were, but we had to laugh. Not all of his projects were a success, though. Once, he put up some new curtain rails – the latest things, where you pulled a cord and the curtains swished shut. When it came to the big demo, he pulled the cord and the whole thing fell down, curtains, runner and all. Oh well – back to the drawing board.

Nicola and Andrew bought a house in readiness for their wedding, so they were kept busy arranging things for the house and the big day. Jason was now spending some time in a wheelchair as opposed to lying in bed all the time; we were hoping that he would be able to come out of hospital for the wedding.

We heard from Liz and Dave, who were moving house again. They would soon have moved as many times as us. They promised that they would come to the wedding. Dave did more home improving than Bill – he was a bit more daring, though. He would think nothing of climbing on the roof and replacing any loose tiles or even windows. He would spend months on a property, then just when it looked immaculate they would sell up and start all over again.

Nicola's wedding day arrived, and it was not such a good day – not weatherwise, anyway. There was rain and wind and then

Diamonds in the Coal Dust

more rain, but everything went more or less according to plan. Flo and Tom made it to the wedding service, but Bill and I took them home immediately afterwards as Tom was not too well and didn't feel like coming up to the reception. We then went on to the reception where the photographer had already begun to take photographs, but the wind was not being very kind to him. Nicola's veil was flying up in the air, and at one point my hat flew off my head and bowled round the car park before being retrieved. Nicola and her bridesmaids looked beautiful, but I have to say that we were not too impressed with the photographer. One of the best photographs we have of that day is one that Bill took at the reception of the couple cutting their wedding cake; they had the image blown up to poster size. We were pleased that Jason made it to the wedding. He returned to the hospital afterwards.

Bill was now suffering more acutely with his old back problem. He had been to see a specialist, but they said that there was not a lot that they could do; there was just too much wear and tear. He learned to recognise his limitations, but he did get very frustrated.

Martin had met a young girl and they seemed to be getting along like a house on fire. She was a hairdresser. Ann and Jason's relationship was coming apart a little. He was being rehabilitated, and they were thinking of getting a house together which would have to be adapted – it was not going to be straightforward. Ann was still working at the chemist's in the village, but I think she was finding it difficult to cope.

There was talk among some friends of a sponsored parachute jump, and two or three of us, including Nicola, said that we would have a go. Bill was not too keen on me doing it and even Martin tried to talk me out of it. He told me that I would have to take my dentures out. 'But why?' I asked him. 'Well, as you scream when you jump out of the plane, your dentures will fly out,' he said. That did worry me, but I decided I would just have to concentrate on keeping my mouth shut for once. As the day dawned, I was the only one jumping among the volunteers, but I wasn't scared. At the airfield where I was to do the jump, it was decided that as I wasn't young (cheek) and as I was on my own, it might be better if I did a tandem jump. This meant I would be strapped to a qualified member of the parachute club. It sounded good to me. So off I went, done up like a dog's dinner in my flying suit, with a fetching leather helmet on my head. I felt like Biggles – I was only missing the white silk scarf. The aeroplane set off – well, they said it was an aeroplane, but it looked more like a sardine tin to me. It had metal sides with rivets all the way along and a big gap in the side of the plane where you either jumped or were pushed out. Someone had already told me that I shouldn't be the last one out, as all you could hear were the screams of the ones who had gone before. I didn't have a choice, though, and my partner and myself were soon the only ones left. We knelt on the floor, looking out of the gap, waiting for the signal to go go go. Out of the plane we flew, the wind hitting my face, and my arms and legs flailing about in all directions. My dentures were very low on my list of priorities; survival was everything. The skydivers who had gone before were floating around us like moths around a flame, and suddenly our chute opened. Our fellow chutists gave us thumbs up and I was smiling. We were floating just like the other 'moths', and it was so beautiful and very quiet. We could see the coastline and the patchwork fields laid out below. My instructor pointed to a yellow circle on the ground below. 'That's what we're aiming for,' he yelled. It looked very small but it grew bigger quite quickly, as we floated nearer and nearer. 'Pull on the handles of the chute hard,' he yelled. I did as I was told and we gently landed on the floor, him on his feet and me on my bum. But we did manage to hit the target! I felt so exhilarated, and after I was unstrapped, I set off to tell Bill – who had been observing us – all about it. 'Oi!' yelled the instructor. 'Pick up the parachute, you have to take it back.' I was floating for several days afterwards, and received a certificate for my pains. It was a fabulous experience.

Ann and Jason had decided to split up. He had gone to live in a bungalow with his brother. It was rather sad, but I think it was the best for both of them.

Martin and his girlfriend had become engaged – we were very surprised, as he had never got that far before. But he was nearly thirty, so we guessed that he was old enough to know his own

Diamonds in the Coal Dust

mind, and he had his own home and was managing very nicely, thank you.

As Bill had more and more time off work with his back trouble, he was seriously considering his future, and when he was offered early retirement from the pit, he decided to go for it.

Being at home with no job was a novelty for him at first. He did a bit of fishing and messed about with his car, but with no jobs left to do in the house, he soon got fed up.

Ann had passed her driving test at the first attempt, and was seeing a man who was a few years older than her. I was still at the school, but was a little bit fed up of the split-shifts. I would prepare the evening meal before I went to my second shift, and ask Bill to switch the pans on at 5.30 p.m. I would arrive home at 6 p.m. and the pans would be boiling merrily away, steam running down the walls. 'Why didn't you turn the heat down?' I would ask Bill, who would have his eyes glued to the TV. 'You never told me to turn them down,' he said – nothing ever changed.

We thought about buying a business that we could run together, to give Bill an interest and to get me away from my job. We did go and look at a few pubs, but they were either too expensive or too run-down, plus the fact that Bill liked his beer possibly a bit too much. We looked at several corner shops, although we didn't know much about the running of one. We finally found one with living accommodation. It was only small, but I think what swung it for Bill was the fact that one of his old fishing mates lived within walking distance of the shop. I didn't mind too much, as I suspected that most of the running of it would fall to me anyway, and Bill did need his fishing as a hobby.

We put the house on the market, and really hadn't a clue how it would go, as none of the houses had been sold previously. It sold within two weeks, and it looked like we would be moving around Christmas time.

The couple who were selling the shop were retiring and had obviously given up on the business; it was quite run-down, but a positive challenge.

As time passed, it looked as if the move was going to be just after Christmas. The vendors were pushing for a completion, but as we had missed the Christmas trade, I thought that it would be better to leave it until after the festive season.

The lady of the shop was ringing us at regular intervals to pester us for an earlier completion. In the end I had to tell her that if she did not stop harassing us, we would pull out of the deal.

Over the Christmas holidays, we packed everything up, ready for the off. We couldn't even have the Christmas tree up, which I did not like one bit – one of the highlights of Christmas for me was digging out the tree and all the decorations. The moving day was actually on 4 January, and on New Year's Eve we had a few drinks with our neighbours. It was sad to say goodbye to them, but we knew that we would be keeping in touch.

Bill and Paddy, one of our neighbours, got into the whisky, and when that was gone they started on the brandy, but I think that Bill had the biggest share. At some stage in the proceedings Bill went upstairs to the toilet. He climbed the stairs to go up, but came back down on his backside. Fortunately there was a very large cardboard box at the bottom of the stairs, already packed with bedding. It was a perfect cushion for him, but sadly the box split under the onslaught, and all four corners gave way. Bill just lay there like a beached whale, grinning from ear to ear. It took the three of us to haul him up onto his feet again.

On 4 January, moving day, it was raining cats and dogs, and I watched my lovely carpet become muckier by the minute as many feet walked back and forth, transporting boxes and furniture. We had plenty of willing helpers, and even Dave turned up to give us a hand.

We had already decided to close the shop for a few days to give it a damned good going-over; that was a good decision, as when we actually got into the shop, we were not pleased. Apart from the fact that it was not too clean, there was hardly any stock on the shelves. We quickly realised that was the reason why they had wanted to move out before Christmas. They had obviously let their stock run down, thinking that they would be gone before the Christmas rush.

Good old Dave came, and he and Bill set to putting up new shelving and generally gutting the place. I found an old cardboard box behind the counter which was full of old cigarette ends.

Diamonds in the Coal Dust

Obviously someone had been smoking in the shop and just chucked the dog-ends in the box, probably when a customer came in.

Bill and Dave did a great job, even ripping up the grotty old floor covering and repainting the walls. The only problem was that when one of them was outside the shop sawing wood for the shelves, they found that people were trying to get into the shop, and they had to explain that it wasn't yet open. The whole place looked so much lighter and brighter when it was finished; we were quite pleased with the transformation. The day before we were due to open, we went to the cash and carry and bought loads of stock. We had to learn as we went along, but we managed. As there was no stock to talk of when we took over, we tried out different things each time we went to the cash and carry. Some things were a success and some things were not; our customers were mostly regulars and had to be coaxed into trying something different. We ourselves did not like the cheap-brand stuff that I think the previous owners had relied on, so, along with some of the budget brands, we introduced more famous brands as well.

We opened seven days a week, but on Sundays we closed for lunch, the only day that we did. We would never have had anything to eat otherwise, as Sundays were manic. But through the week it was quite steady: morning would be lively, when people were going to work and children going to school. Then there would be a quiet couple of hours, then the lunchtime rush, another steady couple of hours and then the usual rush up to closing time. I did the books weekly and sometimes Bill would go off to the cash and carry on his own, but usually we would both go after the shop was closed. Bill was not too keen on being in the shop by himself, as he wasn't too good at small talk. Bill would sometimes have the odd day off to go fishing and catch up with his mates, but it was a very busy time.

We built up a reasonably steady trade and I think that, considering we were new to it, we did quite well. We sold lots of cigarettes and sweets, but really we were willing to try anything that we were asked for. A big helping of patience was needed, especially when two or three kids came in with ten pence to spend; we had an assortment of tuck-shop sweets mostly costing one penny each, and it sometimes took a long time for the kids to make those big decisions.

Nicola and Andrew were looking round for a bigger house, but it was at the end of the '80s, during the housing boom, and houses were being snapped up at an alarming rate. They had been told by a couple of their friends that there was still one house up for sale on a new development, where their friends had already bought one. It was quite a nice development of detached four-bedroomed houses, so that was Nicola and Andrew fixed up. On a visit to see them, when they told us about their new house, we were looking through their property guides, and I saw an advert for a house in a little village quite near to where we lived. As we would be almost driving past on our way home, we decided to check it out. It looked very dingy and unloved, but it did look as though it had some potential. We decided to close the shop for lunch the next day and made an appointment to go and view it. Yes, it was detached, but it looked very run-down from the outside.

Inside there was an L-shaped kitchen with a Rayburn, and a huge lounge/diner with an open staircase and a built-in bar in the corner. Upstairs, there were two bedrooms and a massive bathroom with a sunken corner bath, a separate shower cubicle and a toilet. We didn't say much to the lady who owned the house, but as we drove back to the shop I could tell that Bill was itching to get his hands on the house and turn it into something special. We had a talk about it – what there was to talk about? – we knew that we wanted it. After the cramped living conditions of the shop's accommodation, it would feel like a mansion. We put in an offer the next morning and it was accepted. We thought that Bill could go over to the house each morning and get to work, and I could go through each evening when the shop was closed. It took five or six weeks, and then the house was ours. It really was in an awful state. The foam-backed carpets were stuck to the floor, and the curtains were hung like bits of string at the windows. But it was just so big! Bill's first job was to chuck the old carpets and curtains out through the door – they were so smelly. There had been an old truck standing out at the front of the house which dripped oil everywhere. Bill had the time of his

Diamonds in the Coal Dust

life throwing out everything that wasn't nailed down. When the shop was closed, I would go through to join him. Sometimes I would take a meal I had prepared, or sometimes I could call for a takeaway. We had a couple of chairs there, and a TV – it was great, just like camping out.

Martin and Kate were busy organising their wedding, and Ann had moved in with her boyfriend, so there were just the two of us. Sometimes on Sundays, Martin and his fiancée would take over in the shop so that we had a day off, or sometimes it would be Nicola and Ann. We had decided that once the house was ready we would live in it and travel to the shop each day. It was exciting, seeing the house emerge from the dark, dingy place that it had been to the bright, light place that it was to become. The walls and ceilings had been painted, the bedrooms wallpapered and, best of all, new carpets fitted. The transformation was unbelievable.

We had been gradually taking pieces of furniture, so that we had more and more of our personal stuff at the new house and less on the shop premises.

Martin's wedding went off very well and it was a glorious day. They were to live in Martin's house in Wetherby.

We had also received some extraordinary news – Ann and Howard were expecting a baby. What a lovely surprise, and totally out of the blue. I was going to be a grandparent! This was turning out to be quite a momentous year. There was one low point, however. My friend Flo's husband, Tom, had passed away after years of ill health. He was a lovely man. What would Flo do without him? That I did not know.

The shop was doing well, and we had built up quite a trade since taking over. Bill had lost interest in the shop since buying the house, but Ann's news was something to look forward to. Most of our customers lived quite close to the shop, so that we got to know some of them quite well. One elderly lady who was a regular told me that she was looking forward to her daughter and grandson coming from Australia. We later learned that her daughter had actually split up from her husband in Australia and was coming back to live with her mum.

Ann's baby was due in January, and we were busy preparing

for that event. Ann was in good health during her pregnancy fortunately – not like my pregnancies.

A few months down the line, the lady who had returned from Australia asked us if we would be interested in selling the shop. She said that she had been brought up in the area and had always had a hankering after it. Of course, Bill thought that it was a brilliant idea; we could move lock, stock and barrel into the house and enjoy it. The sale only took a matter of weeks before it was all done and dusted.

We had a brilliant Christmas with all the family – it was such a luxury, having so much room. We invited Charlie, the elderly gent who had the house next to us and who lived by himself, and of course Flo came to join in with the rest of our family.

Bill was not a gracious receiver of presents, and he was slightly embarrassed when it came to the opening ceremony. He would usually say to me, 'You open it for me, I can't be bothered.' That year, Martin surpassed himself. He would usually get his dad something jokey, but this time he handed Bill his present and we all burst out laughing. The wrapping paper had a pattern which read, 'Happy Christmas, you miserable old b—d.' Bill saw the funny side of it and told Martin to 'bugger off'. It was a lovely Christmas, with everybody joining in and no falling out.

On 15 January, my beautiful granddaughter Hollie was born. I could not wait to see her and I was off the minute that I received word. Ann wanted to be out of hospital as soon as possible, but she had to wait until she got the all-clear. A last-minute examination showed that the baby had a slight heart murmur, but the doctor said that it was quite common and they made an appointment for six months down the line. She was such a good baby – no trouble at all – so it was a shock when she went back for a check-up. They referred her to a heart specialist at Killingbeck Hospital. It was discovered that she had a serious heart problem, called Tetralogy of Fallot, and would need major heart surgery at some point in the future. It was hard to believe – she was such a happy little girl.

Ann and Howard, meanwhile, had decided to get married. Ann had always wanted the works, with the floaty dress and pretty

Diamonds in the Coal Dust

bridesmaids. Nicola by this time had been married four years and Martin two years. Ann knew just what she wanted, so the plans were made easy. She had decided to get married from our house.

The weather was not very kind – in fact, it threw it down in the morning – but it had cleared up a bit by the time we left for the service. Ann's friend was in charge of Hollie until after the formal proceedings. She was dressed in a mini version of Ann's dress, white with pale pink trim, and the bridesmaids were also in pink and white. It was a very pretty wedding, and one of the highlights for me was when Ann held Hollie for a photograph. Hollie looked up at her mum with the veil and headdress, as if to say, 'Do I look as silly as you?'

When Hollie was a year old, we were surprised by the news that Nicola and Andrew were expecting a baby. Nicola had never seemed to think much about having children and was doing very well at work. Nicola worked all the way through her pregnancy, but when she was seven months pregnant, she was rushed into hospital with suspected pre-eclampsia and there she had to stay until her baby was born. She had obviously been trying to do too much.

After nearly four weeks in hospital, my grandson was born. He was delivered by caesarean section and he was gorgeous. His name was Elliot.

When Hollie started walking and became more active, her disability began to affect her more and more. The least exertion would leave her gasping for breath. She would walk a few steps and then squat down on the floor until she got her breath back. Each time that she went to Killingbeck for her check-up, it was always the same answer: 'She is on the waiting list.'

Ann and Howard moved into a bungalow quite near to Nicola and Andrew, and, shortly after, Ann became pregnant with her second baby. When Jessica was born, Hollie was so ill that she spent most of her time either in the high chair or in her pushchair. At Howard's place of work, the personnel officer asked to see him. As there were some redundancies in the offing, Howard feared the worst. However, she actually asked him about Hollie and said that she might be able to help. She wanted to know whether they would be prepared to take Hollie to Great Ormond

Street Hospital, to be considered for an operation there. Howard and Ann couldn't believe it when two weeks later they were off to London so that Hollie could be checked out. They were there three days while the doctors assessed the extent of her problems – they then said that they could operate in the next month. It was unbelievable, but wonderful.

Great Ormond Street had a flat where parents of sick children could stay, so that they could be near their children for however long it took.

Nicola said that she would look after Jessica, as she was already at home with Elliot. We stayed by the telephone from the time we knew that Hollie was due to have her operation. Ann rang afterwards to say that it was all over and that Hollie was in intensive care. We breathed a sigh of relief, and phoned all the relatives, who were anxiously waiting for news. I think we thought that the worst was over, but then Hollie got an infection and from there on it was a rollercoaster. One day she would be picking up, and then there would be another infection. They didn't seem to be able to find anything to combat the infections. Ann was missing Jessica, so it was arranged that Nicola would drive to London to take Jessica to stay with her mum and dad. We were very worried about Hollie, as she was a very sick little girl, so we were very relieved when Ann rang us to say that Hollie had turned the corner. All the parents there whose children had undergone similar operations had struck up friendships, and were supporting each other, but sadly, one little boy did not make it. The following weekend Nicola said that she was going down to London and that I could go with her to see Hollie. Ann had assured me that she was greatly improved, so I had set myself up for a happy reunion. But when I went in to see her, I was shocked – she looked like a little old lady, with tubes everywhere. I knew that I was going to cry. Ann took me to one side and said, 'Don't cry in front of Hollie, it will upset her.'

'But you said she was doing great,' I said. Ann explained that she was great compared to how she had been a few days before.

Once she got on her feet, though, Hollie never looked back. Nicola and I trimmed the bungalow up with banners and balloons on the day she was due home; it was a good day. It was

Diamonds in the Coal Dust

good to see Hollie with pink lips, trotting round without having to stop for breath.

Elliot was a lovely happy boy, quite content to sit and play with his toys. Jessica, on the other hand, was not content to sit anywhere at any time. She was a real live wire, and she would not be restrained in any way. She could unfasten the straps of her car seat at a very young age, and could climb out of her cot before she could walk. Ann has a photograph of her in her bedroom; she had climbed out of her cot, pulled the drawer front off her bedroom unit, piled all her clothes in the middle of the floor, and fallen asleep on top of the pile. Hollie was two years older than her, but anything Hollie could do, so could Jessica – even if it was roller-skating or riding a bike – she was fearless.

When Hollie was four and Jessica was two, Ann's third little girl was born. Laura was different again to the other two. To start with, she was a big girl, not built for speed, but very placid and quite content to sit and watch the world go by.

When Laura was seven weeks old, Ann and Howard took the two older girls away for a holiday in the sun. Laura was left with Bill and me, but apart from feeding and changing her, we had little to do; she was not a minute's trouble.

At Christmas, we would usually go to watch the children open their presents, and Howard would be there with the video camera. I was usually in trouble, as I always wrapped my presents extra well, and it would take the kids so long to get inside them that Howard would have to turn the video camera off until they had almost managed to get inside the parcel. It became a standing joke that if anyone was having a problem getting inside their gift, there would be a shout of, 'That's from Grandma!'

We had been having problems with the Rayburn; whenever it was windy, the kitchen would fill with smoke. It was found that a plate at the back of the oven was cracked. We decided to have it taken out, have a gas supply installed and a gas boiler put in for the central heating. That was the signal for Bill to get busy again with the old DIY.

The lounge and dining room were such a huge space as one that it was difficult to keep the whole place warm in winter. He put a partition wall up between the two rooms, then knocked a doorway through the wall from the kitchen into the dining room.

The ever-faithful Dave came up with a good idea. As we didn't have a window looking out onto the garden, he suggested that they knock a hole in the wall in the lounge, and put a window in. What a brilliant idea – it was surprising what a difference it made. Good old Dave.

We received a letter from Chris and Mona to tell us that they were coming for a holiday. Apparently, Chris had been driving them both to the supermarket, and they had had an accident in which Mona's shoulder was injured. Mona had claimed for her injury from his insurance and, with the money that she got, they were coming for a holiday. They were to stay this time with their son quite near to where Flo lived. At some point, we were going to meet up with them and hopefully they would be spending some time with us. I had been to take Flo shopping, as I did each week, when we came across Chris and Mona – she really didn't look well at all. She told me that she had a bad chest, and was going to see the doctor. I told them that I would give them a ring to arrange for us to get together. However, I soon got a call from Chris to tell me that Mona was in hospital; they had found a problem and had to remove one of her lungs. What bad luck to have on holiday, but I suppose it would have happened if they had been in Australia. I picked Chris up a couple of times and took him to the hospital to see Mona. She looked frail, as you would expect. After a couple of weeks she came out of hospital, and eventually arrangements were made for them to go back to Australia. We all went to the airport to see them off. Mona was in a wheelchair and I think that I wasn't the only one who thought that we might never see her again.

I rang a couple of times after they went home and had a word with Mona. She said that she was OK, but tired. But a couple of weeks later, I had a letter from Chris to say that Mona was going to Sydney for some tests, as she was having pains in her back. There, they discovered that there was nothing they could do, and Mona went into a hospice where she died quite quickly. I did feel sorry for Chris, as, even though he had family out there, he was more or less on his own.

Diamonds in the Coal Dust

After a few months he wrote that he was coming to England to bring Mona's ashes – we were pleased about that. When he came to see us, Liz and Dave arrived one day. It was a real tonic for Chris, as Liz was always good for a laugh; she told Chris that she would marry him when she divorced Dave. I have some treasured photographs of that day, taken in the garden. He went back to Australia shortly afterwards, and we wondered whether we would ever see him again.

Bill's mum and dad were not getting any younger. His mum had been having a problem with her breathing. A couple of trips to the hospital showed that she had fluid on one of her lungs. Twice she went and had her lung drained, but it always seemed to fill up again. An appointment was made for her to see a specialist. I went with her, and the specialist told her that they had found something on her lung but unfortunately it was in such a place that they could not do anything about it. She did not seem at all phased about it and I wondered whether perhaps she had not fully understood, but I think maybe she knew. I told Bill what the specialist had said, and he thought that perhaps we should not say anything to his dad.

As the weeks went on, she struggled more and more and it was decided that perhaps someone should be there through the night. Bill's brother said that he would do one week if we did the other – he was working at the time. So that's what we did between us. In the end she was virtually bedridden, and had lost such a lot of weight. She had always been such an active, hard-working lady all her life. Her garden was always a picture and, between her and Bill's father, they kept themselves in vegetables from the back garden. There was also always an array of soft fruit, which was bottled and baked and kept in store for the months ahead.

Two weeks before Christmas, it was my and Bill's week to cover. I saw his mum and dad to bed and gave her the medication. Early the next morning, I heard his dad moving about. Bill got up, made himself a cup of coffee and left to go home as he usually did. I took his mum a cup of tea while his dad went downstairs to get his array of tablets. Upstairs, his mum was breathing really heavily. I looked out of the window to wave to Bill as he drove round the corner, and suddenly everything went very quiet. I went over to her and knew immediately that she had passed away. I ran downstairs to Bill's dad and asked him if he would go and sit with her while I rang for the doctor. Of course, he was very upset and rubbed her hand and tried to talk to her. I took the pillow away from her head, so that she was lying flat, and told him that she wasn't very well and just to sit with her while I phoned for the doctor. The doctor came almost at once, telling Bill's dad that it was all over. I rang Bill's brother, who of course was at work, but his wife said that she would ring him at work immediately. I then phoned Bill and asked him to come straight back to his mum's. His dad of course went to pieces, and was not at all pleased when he learned that she had had cancer; but she hadn't wanted him to know, and who were we to question that decision?

After her funeral, Bill's dad went to spend Christmas with his daughter, who lived quite a distance away. He came back home after a month, and managed quite well. Different members of the family kept an eye on him and he pottered about in the garden, but not with the same commitment as before.

Just over a year later, Bill had taken his dad out for a drink on the Friday night, as he sometimes did. Bill said that they had had a good laugh – in fact, Bill said that he was still laughing when he took him home. On the Sunday morning, Bill's brother rang to see whether his dad was with us, as his neighbour had noticed that his curtains were still closed. We told him that we hadn't seen him since Friday night, so Bill's brother went to investigate, and found that his dad had died while he was getting dressed. It was as quick as that – he obviously hadn't known anything about it.

So that was the end of another era. Martin was particularly upset, as he had always been close to his grandma and granddad, as he had been to Edie B.

Chapter Eight

Nicola wanted to go back to work, so I was to look after Elliot. It was a bit of a journey from where we lived to Nicola's, but he was a good kid.

We bought a static caravan on the coast; several of our friends were already on the same site. Bill loved it. We were on the cliff top, and we would lie in bed and hear the waves crashing. It was an old van, but it had a toilet in it and Bill put a shower cubicle in. The kids loved to visit in the school holidays.

When Elliot was three years old, Nicola and Andrew put him in prep school. I will never forget his first day. He had a green blazer, grey trousers – which met up with his three-quarter socks over his little chubby knees – and a green cap with a badge on. He was just a baby, but he loved it. He had only been there a few months when he won a prize for one of his paintings. He was a very clever little boy.

One day a week, I would go to Ann's to see the girls. Laura was a happy smiley child, but didn't seem in a hurry to walk. Ann began to wonder whether there was a problem – she thought that one of Laura's legs seemed to be slightly shorter than the other. She was sent to hospital to see a specialist, and it was thought that she had a very slight curvature of the spine. She was also asymmetrical, with one side of her slightly different to the other. That explained why she had difficulty keeping her balance. The specialist did not think it would be a long-term problem and said that she would probably grow out of it. As it happened, she did start toddling around nineteen months of age, and although she was a bit on the clumsy side, she was fine.

Ann's daughters were three lovely girls, all different. Hollie was fair and slim and amiable, Jessica was dark with lovely brown eyes and sharp as a tack, and Laura was loveable, cuddly and generous to a fault. She would give anyone her last Rolo. I had been to Ann's on one of my weekly visits, and we took the girls out for a walk. Ann was pushing Laura in the buggy and I was walking behind with the other two. On our way home, it started to rain cats and dogs. We rushed home, but still managed to get soaking wet. I grabbed a towel and started to rub Hollie's hair as she hung it down in front of me. Suddenly, she flung her long hair back and snapped her head up, whacking me on the bridge of the nose.

I heard it crack and saw stars before my eyes started watering, and my face began throbbing. Ann realised that something was wrong and came to ask if I was OK. I felt so bad but I knew that I had to get in the car and drive home before things got any worse.

I really don't know how I made it home; I could feel my eyes closing by the minute. When I arrived home, Bill asked me what had happened and, when I told him, all he said was, 'Well, there's no point in going to the doctor's, as they can't do anything for a broken nose.' I couldn't have cared less – all I wanted to do was go to bed and feel sorry for myself.

I didn't go out for a few days, as I looked as though I had done ten rounds with Mike Tyson. My eyes were every colour of the rainbow and half shut, but after a few days, even though it looked bad, it wasn't all that painful. Poor old Hollie – yes, she did break my nose, but it was a total accident.

Sadly, Martin and his wife decided to separate. I don't know whose fault it was, but it happened. They had sold the house which Martin had bought in Wetherby, and had signed up for a new build which would be some months in construction. In the meantime they had gone to live with Martin's sister-in-law and her husband. Whether that had contributed to the break-up, who knows. Martin was stuck with the new house, as he had signed the contract and couldn't afford to pull out. I did feel for Martin but was confident that he would come through; he was a good lad.

When Elliot was four, his father left the family. He had been working down south and coming home for the weekends. Then he would miss a weekend, and then another, until Nicola didn't know if or when he was coming home. So came the parting of the waves. I felt so sorry for Elliot – how could his father not want to

Diamonds in the Coal Dust

see him? Nicola kept up with her job, and eventually got a transfer to a branch down south in Slough.

The house was put on the market and she set about finding a place to buy. As her house was sold quite quickly, she found an apartment to rent in a place near Slough that would be handy for her new workplace. Bill and I helped to pack up. Andrew turned up with a van to collect the stuff that he was claiming, but didn't help with anything else.

We drove down with Nicola and Elliot to Langley, where they were renting for the time being. The apartment was in a lovely building; it was very spacious and in a very nice area.

Nicola settled in well at her new workplace and set about looking for a place to buy, as she had rented the apartment for just six months. Elliot seemed to have settled into school and had already found a little friend.

After they had been down south for four months or so, Nicola was pleased to tell us that she had found somewhere to buy. It was an older semi in nearby Slough, quite near to Elliot's school. She assured Bill that it was a bargain, as properties in Slough were snapped up in no time; indeed, two more prospective buyers were snapping at Nicola's heels. But as she was not in a chain she had priority. The only fly in the ointment was the fact that the house needed gutting. She would have to stay in the apartment until most of the work was done.

Bill and I went down so that Bill could give it the once-over. He was horrified when he saw it, and reckoned they should have paid Nicola to take it on.

Before she could move in with Elliot, it had to be re-wired, damp-proofed, and have central heating and double glazing installed. It had obviously not been lived in for a long time, as the garden was like a wilderness. Near the back door, a vine had leapt from the garage roof to the house, and threatened to strangle anyone who tried to get round the back of the house. That said, it was a lovely house and, if you looked beyond all the work that needed doing, it had bags of potential. The back garden was quite a size, with a cherry tree, a plum tree and several apple trees. But despite all that, Bill was still not impressed. I think that if he had been younger and fitter and could have spent some considerable time there, he would have been happier.

We went down again when it was considered safe enough for them to move into. We helped to pack up their stuff at the apartment and on the actual moving day, Nicola hired a box van to move her big stuff. Quite a lot of things had already been transported in Bill's car and Nicola's. It was only a three-mile journey, so they could get there and back in no time. It was the usual Mum-and-Dad-and-Nicola fiasco – with Bill, you were not allowed to have fun when dealing with any situation; it all had to be taken very seriously. This was something that Nicola and I found very difficult – as a result, we were always in trouble for laughing.

The apartment was in a Georgian-type building, with lawn all the way round. There was just a footpath to the main door, and vehicles had to be parked up and could not be driven up to the doors. The furniture had to be hauled down the footpath to the van. Bill was of course the foreman and stood on the tailgate of the van, urging Nicola and me on every step of the way. We staggered down the drive with chests of drawers, the settee and chairs, and when we reached the van, we had to heave the furniture up so that Bill could place it in the back of the van. We managed quite well until we were struggling with a double mattress; it was the deepest, heaviest mattress I had ever seen or handled. We huffed and puffed with this mattress and by the time we reached the van we were shattered. Bill was urging us on from the back of the van: 'Lift it up, lift it higher.' The more he shouted and the redder his face got, the more we collapsed with laughter – we giggled so much that we could not do anything. 'Stop laughing, you silly buggers, and lift it up!' he yelled. I swear it was the only mattress that had grass stains on it. How we managed everything without doing ourselves a mischief I will never know. We finally managed to move all the big stuff before the van had to be returned for closing time. We thought that Bill would offer to take it back, but no such luck. So Nicola, who was only small, climbed up into this clapped-out van and I went along with her for moral support – not that I was a lot of good. So there we were, perched up in this old van... Nicola couldn't get it in gear, and we clanked and screeched and backfired all the way through the streets. When we arrived, the chap said, 'Can you put it round

Diamonds in the Coal Dust

here?' Nicola jumped out and said, 'I'm leaving it right here; you can put it where you like.' We laughed all the way back to the house.

There were no carpets down or anything, as Nicola was having a new kitchen fitted and everywhere redecorated eventually. At least she was in, and it was her own place.

Elliot's room was the priority, so that he would feel settled. The rest of it would take much longer.

Our fortieth wedding anniversary was now coming up. We didn't plan to have a formal do; it was lovely weather, so we decided to have a buffet party at the caravan. We put long tables down the length of the van, and asked our caravan friends to bring their own chairs. It was a lovely day. Bill's brother and his wife came, as did Liz and Dave (I was pleased about that), Flo, Ann and her family, Marie (one of my old school friends) and her husband. Nicola and Elliot couldn't make it, and Martin was at a football match, but there were lots of our caravan friends. I had made quite a spread and of course there was plenty of booze. I couldn't believe that it was forty years since we were married – I did wonder what I had been doing for the last forty years!

It was a lovely friendly atmosphere at the caravan site; everybody knew each other, and Bill liked nothing better than to potter about. All the men would congregate together and have a natter like old women. For myself, I loved to walk along the sea front into the little town, and potter around the shops. I would probably buy a bag of freshly made doughnuts and eat most of them before I got back to the van.

It was while we were at the caravan for one of our weekends that we learned about the death of Princess Diana. It was Sunday morning, and I was used to getting up quite early to go and get a newspaper. I switched on the television and saw the headlines: 'Princess Diana is dead!' It also showed the mangled remains of the car, and at first I thought that a bomb had blown it up. I ran into the bedroom shouting to Bill, 'They've killed Diana!' Bill had been asleep but came running into the lounge, where we sat listening to the news. I was devastated. I loved Diana to bits and thought that she had had a raw deal from the royal family, especially from her ex-husband. We set off for home – I don't know why, I just wanted us to be at home to catch any news as it had happened.

I had telephoned Nicola as soon as I heard the news, but she had just switched on her TV and seen it for herself. She was as devastated as I was; we had followed the Diana story from the time she was seen on TV with the sun shining through her dress at the nursery where she worked. I had never been a fan of Prince Charles (preferring Princess Anne), but when it appeared that he had fallen in love with Diana, he went up in my estimation – though not for long. I think that I began to have doubts during their engagement interview, when he said those very well-quoted words, 'whatever love means', when he was asked by the interviewer if he was in love. It seemed such a spiteful and childish thing to say. Of course, we learned the truth much later – that he had never been in love with Diana; she was just a means to an end. The truth of the matter was that she was too good for him and deserved better. After the break-up of their marriage, Diana's character assassination began, with 'the firm' manipulating the press to make 'poor old Charles' look like the victim. A proper Charlie, more like.

I only watched Diana's funeral in parts – I just found it too upsetting. I did tape it, but to this day I have not watched it in full. The week after the funeral, I went down south to spend some time with Nicola and we decided to go into London to 'do' Diana's flowers. I wouldn't have missed it for anything. It was the most moving experience that I have ever witnessed. There were thousands of people milling about in absolute silence, with people laying flowers and reading the hundreds of cards, notices and other tributes. At least, or at last, she was getting the respect that she deserved.

We did have one very strange experience the next day. Nicola's friend, Susie, picked us up in her car in the early morning, as we were going to a nearby market. She asked us if we would like to try to find the cemetery where Dodi was buried; she knew the area, but didn't know exactly where it was. We drove round and round with no success and had almost decided to give it up as a bad job. Suddenly, a limousine with darkened windows appeared

Diamonds in the Coal Dust

in front of us – the number plate read DODI. We couldn't believe it, and Susie set off after it. We lost sight of it in the flow of traffic, but when we approached a roundabout, the car came from the right of us. Again we set off after it and we hadn't gone very far when Susie yelled, 'There's the cemetery.' We turned off the road at the signpost (the limousine didn't) and there we were at the cemetery. There was hardly anybody there – just a security guard and two or three other people besides us. We all stood for a few moments. It was very peaceful, with gently piped music being played. We said a little prayer and quietly left, but we were still bewildered by the circumstances that had brought us to that unique place.

I believe that shortly afterwards Mr Al Fayed took Dodi to be buried on his estate.

That weekend was an emotionally draining experience, but I was glad to have been there.

Chapter Nine

We had a letter from Chris in Australia, telling us that he wasn't too well. He had been having trouble with his breathing and was finding it difficult to manage on his own. He was thinking of going to live with his daughter, who had moved to Queensland. He was in his 80s and, since Mona died, had been struggling a bit. He gave up his house and Lynn, his daughter, came for him and took him back with her up to Queensland. He hadn't been there very long when I received a letter. Chris had dictated it, but Lynn had written it. He told me in the letter that he was going into a nursing home, as he was worried that it would be too much for Lynn to look after him, because she worked full-time. He said that he would write to me when he was settled in the home. But less than two weeks later I received another letter from Lynn to say that Chris had died; his heart had given up. I was so sad, as we had had some laughs together, and he had been such a happy little man.

Bill was finding it difficult doing the jobs and maintenance needed on a regular basis to an old property. It was decided that we would sell the house and buy a bungalow. I would be sad to leave that house, as I had enjoyed living there. The house had been on the market for a few weeks with not much interest, but one day Bill had gone fishing and I was ironing when I received a phone call. A gentleman was outside the house and had seen the For Sale sign. He wanted to know whether he could have a look around; of course, I said that he could. He came in and looked round and within five minutes he had left. I went back to my ironing, but thirty minutes later the estate agent rang and said that the man wanted the house and had offered the full asking price. When Bill came home, I had to tell him that we had sold the house.

That meant panic stations, as we hadn't bothered looking for anything up until then. We picked out three bungalows to look at.

Diamonds in the Coal Dust

The first one was filthy – not that we minded some decorating, but they hadn't even tidied it up. The second one was a new one which had been empty for twelve months; it was very nice and we put in an offer, but it was rejected, so that left number three. I really wasn't impressed with it; for my part, it just wasn't big enough, especially after the house we were leaving. However, we had to downsize and we had to get out of our house, as the man who was buying it wanted an early completion. So that's how we came to be in our bungalow.

There were two bedrooms but no dining room, so the second bedroom had to double as a dining room. The bungalow was certainly easier for Bill – a bit too easy, as he soon became bored. Nicola managed to get him a reconditioned computer and he set about teaching himself how to use it.

I kept myself busy going to see the kids and Flo, and I had a day out usually once a week.

Liz rang to say that Dave was in hospital. The doctor thought that he had had a stroke. She rang again a couple of days later to tell us that they were thinking of discharging him. Liz was panicking, wondering how she would manage him, as she said that he needed caring for and was partially paralysed. Poor old Dave.

She need not have worried, as the next day Dave's daughter rang me to tell me that her dad had passed away. It was probably for the best, as Dave was such an active man that he wouldn't have wanted to be anything less than fully fit.

Martin and I went to his funeral. Bill didn't go, as he had a total aversion to funerals. I could understand that – what's to like about them?

As I mentioned, Bill was busy teaching himself the rudiments of the computer world; he was really taken up with it, and would spend hours with it. The trouble was that if he had a problem he would ring Nicola at work and ask her what he should do. She would ask him, 'Which buttons did you press?' Bill would reply, 'Well, I didn't know what to do, so I pressed everything.' Then Nicola would talk him through his problem and the procedure to get him back on track.

Ann started working at a local estate agent so in the school holidays I would have a houseful, as I usually had Elliot for the holidays.

Flo and I had arranged to go on holiday. Bill said that it was nothing in his line, so she and I booked to go to Majorca for a week followed by a week cruising round the Med. Flo wasn't too good on her feet, so I thought that this holiday would be quite relaxing for us. Bill was happy to go fishing, coming and going as he liked.

The week in Majorca was fabulous – the hotel was top notch in a quiet little fishing port, with not much activity, but very relaxing. We met up with some very nice people. They had done their holiday the opposite way round to us, going on the cruise for their first week and staying in the hotel for the second week. They assured us that the cruise was going to be equally as nice as the holiday.

The second week of our holiday was pure luxury – because we had booked early, we had been upgraded and the cabin was gorgeous. The food was wall-to-wall and the seating arrangements were well planned. Around our table were eight ladies, consisting of four couples. Breakfast was a full-blown affair, but you could choose a continental breakfast if you preferred. Next would be morning coffee, then lunch was either a buffet on deck or the real McCoy in the restaurant. Afternoon tea was optional depending on how greedy you were, and then you had to rest up before tackling evening dinner. Apparently, there was even a midnight buffet, but we never managed to make it there.

Each day, we visited a different port of call. It was very hectic as we had a guide who held up a little flag – supposedly so that we could follow her, but we must have had the smallest guide in Italy as we had trouble seeing her over the sea of heads bobbing about in front of us. She would set off at a rate of knots, weaving in and out of the traffic. I would be trying to keep up with her, while keeping an eye on Flo. I was terrified of becoming separated from the rest of the group, as I would never have been able to find my way back to the ship. We went to the Coliseum, which was very impressive, to the Vatican, and we saw the Tower of Pisa; all very grand.

One day, I did suggest to Flo that we stay on board and just relax, but she wouldn't hear of it. I was conscious that I was virtually dragging her along, when she walked straight into a lamp

Diamonds in the Coal Dust

post. Her glasses flew off and ended up in two pieces. I was scrabbling about on the floor trying to find the pieces from her spectacles while keeping one eye on the flag, which was fast disappearing with our guide into the distance. Poor old Flo – she couldn't see anything without her glasses. When we got back on board ship, I went with her to the reception desk to ask them whether they had any suggestions as to what to do with them. To be fair to them, they did the best they could, but she ended up looking a bit like Jack Duckworth. The next day we spent on board and it was lovely just to lounge around and watch the world go by.

The last day that we had on board, we had to ourselves. We took the launch to shore and followed a group of passengers, not really knowing where we were going. The other members of the group boarded a train, a really grand affair with two storeys and very clean and shiny, not at all like a British Rail train. When the rest of the group left the train, so did we; we were in Monaco. How brilliant was that?

We went off on our own, meandering around the little market which was filled with freshly picked vegetables – it all looked so appetising.

We had lunch at a little pavement café and then slowly made our way up to the pink palace. I think we enjoyed that day as much as – if not more than – the other days, as it was so relaxing. Flo sat and had her photograph taken, eating an ice cream with the palace in the background. It was magical.

Our final evening dinner was a grand affair, and we all dressed up to the nines. It was a beautiful celebratory meal.

Afterwards, there was the final of a talent competition in one of the concert rooms. We thought that might be entertaining and we took a table right at the front so that we wouldn't miss anything. Nothing could have prepared us for the bill of fare that was on offer. There was obviously a shortage of props, as the same wig was used for two Elvises and one Roy Orbison. To be fair, the show was just for laughs – or I think it was. There was a Doris Day, whom I thought was probably the best, but the final act had us all guessing. This little old lady came limping onto the stage; she had white hair, and her voice was quite thin. Flo and I were trying to decide who she was supposed to be: I though Gracie Fields, and Flo thought Dusty Springfield – as if! The old lady started telling the compère about her qualifications; she lived on a smallholding with ducks, hens, pigs and goodness knows what else. So the compère said to her, 'Who are you going to be tonight, Kath?' She said, without blinking an eye, 'Tonight, Matthew, I'm going to be Shirley Bassey.' 'Shirley Bassey!' we both shrieked. I thought we were going to get thrown out, as we exploded with laughter and we couldn't keep quiet. This little old lady was standing there so seriously, and the audience was actually applauding. But that was nothing compared to when she reappeared as Shirley Bassey. She had Elvis's wig on back to front, chandeliers hanging from her ears and a necklace which nearly reached the floor. When she began singing 'Hey Big Spender', that was it. My face hurt from trying not to laugh – in the end, we had to go before we got thrown out. We never did find out who won. It was probably Shirley Bassey!

That was a good night – a fitting finale to a super holiday (apart from Flo's glasses).

Back at home, Martin had a new girlfriend and seemed to be happy. He had managed to sell his new house and, for the immediate future, was renting a place. Bill was becoming a dab hand with his computer – I was proud of his progress; he was picking things up as he went along, but would still spend hours on it.

When it was millennium New Year's Eve, Nicola came up to spend it with us so that she and Elliot wouldn't be alone that night. We had the bubbly and the poppers and so on, and we decided to play charades. Bill wasn't too keen, but he decided to join in anyway. We wrote down characters from a film or book on bits of paper and put them in a bowl. When it was my turn, I couldn't believe what I was reading. 'Who on earth is Olive Twist?' I asked. Bill was most put out, as we were all laughing. 'It's Oliver Twist,' he explained, but it got the biggest laugh of the night. As midnight struck, we went out to the top of our cul de sac; there were lots of people there, and no wonder – you could see across a big part of Leeds and its suburbs, and everywhere you

Diamonds in the Coal Dust

looked there were fireworks going off. It was the most magical sight, and we were all drinking bubbly and wishing each other a Happy New Year. UNFORGETTABLE.

Chapter Ten

Nicola was looking for another position in human resources, as the office she had worked in since she had moved from Yorkshire would cease to exist in the near future.

She was offered the position of HR Manager with a multinational firm some miles away. The director there had worked with Nicola at the present workplace before taking up a post with his new company. Nicola had some misgivings, as she thought that it might be too big a jump for her job-wise, but she decided to give it a try. She was always fearless and I had no doubts that she would make a fist of it. The new job offered a much bigger pay packet, and a better package altogether. She wasn't too happy with the journey – it was a bit of a long drive – but she decided to look for a property which would be better situated for the job.

Elliot had to change schools, but he had not been too happy at his old one for some time. He was enrolled at Yateley Manor, which was handy for Nicola's workplace and the new home. Nicola had a new man whom she had met at her new workplace. They got on quite well, and Elliot seemed to like him. He decided to sell his house and move in with Nicola and Elliot. The new house had five bedrooms, so there would be room for his two children when they came to stay.

In the cul de sac where our bungalow was situated, most of the residents were retired, and Sunday was car wash day. I spoke to most of the residents as and when I saw them, but I didn't stand about chatting to anybody.

One car-washing Sunday, Bill was exchanging niceties with Norman, who lived opposite. Bill told him that we were going to Spain for a couple of weeks. Norman's wife was Spanish, although she had lived in England for over thirty years. He mentioned that they were going out to Spain at the same time as

Diamonds in the Coal Dust

us. They had an apartment out there and were going to be staying there. As it was just twenty minutes from where we were to be staying, Normal suggested that we go and visit them while we were there. He suggested that we went for a meal, so Bill made a note of his address and phone number, but Bill said that he was not sure whether we would go.

Bill had an idea that we might look around the area, with a view to buying a property out there, but he didn't mention this to Norman.

We were going for two weeks and, as the place we were staying was a little bit out of town, we were going to hire a car. We had two or three days to get our bearings, and then we went to find Torrevieja; their apartment was situated there. We rang the bell outside the building, and Norman called to us through the intercom.

The apartment was really nice, and Maria had done a lovely lunch for us, with salad and pasta and chicken. I didn't know Maria all that well, but we chatted on for quite some time with no awkwardness at all. Norman said, 'After lunch, we have a surprise for you.' I wondered what it was all about. However, after we had finished eating, Norman asked Bill where he had parked the car. Bill told him that it was in the car park. 'Well,' he said, 'is there any chance of you taking us for a ride?' Bill went to fetch the car while I stayed with Maria and Norman.

When we piled into the car, Norman said that he was taking us to see his new house. We were gobsmacked. They told us that Norman was now retired, so they were selling their bungalow and moving to Spain, where Maria still had family.

Norman directed Bill to what looked like a building site – which is what it was, as the house wasn't even started, but they showed us the plot where it would eventually be. We also saw the *piso piloto*, which was the show house. Bill was really impressed with the whole thing; it was in a good area, handy for the town and all amenities. The house had an L-shaped lounge/diner, separate kitchen, downstairs shower room and one bedroom, and a bathroom and two bedrooms upstairs.

When Bill said how taken he was with the whole thing, Maria urged us to think about buying on the same development, as there were still some houses available. Bill didn't like rushing into anything, and told them that he wouldn't dream of signing up for another property until we were sure that we would be able to sell our bungalow. The only thing that I was not too sure about was the fact that the houses were in blocks of four – not even semis – they were called quads, and the builders had obviously realised that they could get four houses in the space of one detached. We did say that we would prefer a detached property.

It was certainly an experience, and we told Norman and Maria that we would be putting our bungalow on the market when we went home. We appreciated the advice that Maria gave us – that we shouldn't buy through an agent – but felt that Maria was in a better position than us to go it alone, as she could speak Spanish and was aware of Spanish legislation. She did offer to help us out with any interpretation, but we preferred to go it alone. We loved the area, though, and assured Norman and Maria that we would definitely be looking for somewhere in that neck of the woods.

Their house was not due to be completed for eight months or so; in the meantime, they had put the apartment up for sale but would be keeping the bungalow until a bit nearer their completion date.

We came back from out holiday loaded with literature, but Bill felt that if we couldn't sell the bungalow it was all pie in the sky. We did our homework – or so we thought – weighing up all the pros and cons, read up on all the likely pitfalls and decided from the brochures which style of house we would like and also which property we could afford.

With our bungalow on the market, we set about going to every exhibition of Spanish properties in our area, and there were plenty of them. According to the brochures, we could afford on our budget a three-bedroomed detached villa; we were willing to settle for two bedrooms if necessary. But we had chosen second and third choices just in case of disappointment.

Bill decided that he was going to learn the language, so he bought a Spanish language course for his computer. He spent hours going over and over the same words. I so admired him for his dedication – I could say *si* and *non*, and that would do me for starters. Bill did not have a natural ear for diction; he would listen to the Spanish coach speaking a certain phrase and then Bill would repeat it. There was an accuracy meter on the bottom of his screen, and if he didn't say it just right, the 'tutor' would tell him to try again until it was repeated correctly. Bill would get very frustrated, as he would think he had said the phrase correctly. He would yell into the microphone, 'I said it like that!' as though there was a little man in there listening to him. I had learned French and German at school and I recognised that if you didn't get the pronunciation just right, it wasn't correct. But he tried so hard, and I had to stop myself from laughing at his exchanges with the man behind the mike.

I had begun to sort things out into what was going with us and what needed to be got rid of. Of course, our big furniture would not be going, with the exception of my grandfather clock and the rocking chair that Bill had bought me, and our personal stuff. Of course, Bill's fishing tackle would be going, along with a bike that he had bought, which he thought would make things easier for him to get about.

The bungalow sold quite quickly and we were able to sell most of the furniture that wasn't going with us. I had a car boot sale and managed to offload quite a lot of the unnecessary things which we had gathered over the years. We were going to live with Nicola for the time being, and, as the house which Martin was renting was quite roomy, with a dining room which Martin did not use, he agreed to store our Spanish things for us until such time as we got going. Nicola took the dining table and chairs, so it would be a bit like home for us. But we did feel like refugees with no home to go to. We hadn't a clue how long it was all going to take, but in our naivety we thought that once we had sold our property and packed up, everything would fall into place.

We booked one of the viewing trips which were extensively advertised; we thought that if we picked one of the more reputable ones, we would be OK. We had had to fill in a form previously, stating what type of property we wanted to look at, the area we preferred and how much we had to spend. Everything was covered, no problem – or so we thought. The trip was to last four days – not long to choose a property, open a bank account, meet the solicitor and choose furniture, but that was the schedule. Nicola and her friend decided to come with us, but it was no holiday. Our rep picked us up at the airport and took us back to the hotel. She arranged to meet us for our evening meal, when she would go through the itinerary with us. From the outset, Nicola was not impressed with the rep, but we tried to keep an open mind. We knew just what we wanted and had told the agent our exact requirements, so we weren't too worried.

The hotel was full of people just like us, divided into groups of four or six. The hotel was quite nice (what we saw of it), but interaction between one group and another was not encouraged, even if the time had been available. The rep stayed until bedtime and left us saying that we would be picked up after breakfast the next morning. After the rep had gone, Nicola pointed out that everybody had bought the rep a drink, without her offering to pay at all; in fact, Nicola called her a 'cheeky bugger'.

We were up bright and early the next morning for breakfast, as the rep was picking us up at 9.30 a.m. It was actually 10 a.m. when she arrived, and all the other groups had been gone some time. She told us that she had had trouble getting a child minder for her daughter. GREAT!

We had the brochure in front of us and expected to be taken to see at least one or two of our three choices. She drove round the countryside, showing us places of interest; Bill told her that we had seen it all before. She took us to a couple of building sites, but they weren't the type of house that we had set our hearts on. When we challenged her, she said that we would have to go many miles inland to get the house we wanted at the price we had quoted.

Nicola was ready for going home, we were more than a little cheesed off and the rep was becoming desperate. She showed us apartments, resales and plenty of other properties that we had no intention of buying. At the end of the day, we decided it was a waste of time – but after the evening meal there was our rep, perched on the end of the bar; this time none of our party supplied her drinks. We did wonder how she had managed to find a babysitter for her daughter. The next day, she tried a different approach and took us to the development where her mother lived.

Diamonds in the Coal Dust

It was dreadful. She decided to call at her mother's to see if her daughter was OK. She came back to us five minutes later and said that her mother's neighbour was selling his house and that her mother had the keys if we wanted to have a look around. I think at that point we realised that we were flogging a dead horse and just wanted to go home.

I think most of the people in the hotel had much the same experience, as there was only one sale among the whole of our party. The whole set-up was so unprofessional. I got the idea that they thought we would be falling over ourselves to buy any property that was presented to us, but they should have been charged with abuse of the trade descriptions act, as the properties and the prices bore no resemblance to what we had been shown.

So it was back to the drawing board. We were not too dispirited, as we were quite comfortable at Nicola's. While we were there, Bill decided to try to finish Nicola's decorating, which she been trying to do herself – but working full-time did not leave her much spare time for such things as decorating. I helped out, and we managed to finish the lounge/dining room, one bedroom and finally the staircase.

We had booked to go on another viewing trip, but this time we knew what to expect and were prepared for all the stalling tactics and the hard sell. Just the two of us were going this time, and we had strict instructions from Nicola to be firm and not to sign up for anything unless we were *absolutely* sure. Bill didn't reassure her when he told her that we were not coming home without buying something! She made me promise that we would talk it over at length with each other before coming to a decision.

From the outset, this trip seemed more organised than the previous one. There were eight of us in our group: a couple from Scotland, a couple from Wales with their daughter and son-in-law, and ourselves. We all got on like a house on fire, but I was slightly worried when I learned that the Scottish couple were after an apartment, which they would use as a holiday home; we obviously wanted a detached and the quartet from Wales were not too fussed about any type of property – they had come with an open mind.

Maddy Worth

Lynne, our rep, did her best and took us to see a variety of properties, but we weren't too enamoured with any of them. All the reps seemed to be pushing a certain type of villa, a quad called the Pedro. Lynne took us to see one which was completed, but there was a small crowd of viewers waiting to get in to look round. Bill was not too pleased with the Pedro anyway, and had a word with Lynne. He told her that we had stressed that we would prefer a detached, and had been assured before we came that there would be a choice available during the trip. Lynne had to admit that at the moment there were none of the ones we had chosen from the brochure available.

This was a big disappointment, but she promised to take us to a new development where there would be some available in the future. However, there wasn't even a show house available to show us what they would look like on completion.

She did take us to see a detached house which was a resale, but as they had added extras to it since it was built it had pushed the purchase price up beyond our reach.

We were all feeling a little deflated, as none of us had seen anything that had excited us. We had been round a couple of places and were enjoying lunch at an outdoor restaurant in Torrevieja; it was a lovely day and we had managed to have a laugh among ourselves. We set off on our travels again feeling much more upbeat, when Lynne spotted a sign for a show house. She suggested that we went to see if there were still some houses available. We were impressed – yes, they were the dreaded quads, but when we went inside we were amazed. There was quite a large lounge/diner, separate kitchen, a beautiful downstairs bathroom and also a double bedroom. Patio doors opened on to a balcony and a large patio led on to double gates.

But, and it was a big but, the outside of the house was so ugly – it was like Stalag 17. I knew that Bill was smitten with it, and to be fair, it was the best house we had seen for the money since we had started looking. Our travel companions were also impressed with this particular property. Lynne asked the agent if there were still some houses available. There were five left out of seventy-six, and Lynne reserved three of them for twenty-four hours, until we made our minds up. All three of them were quite close together, so – if we decided to go for them – we would all be neighbours. They were due to be completed by the following May, which was five to six months ahead, whereas some of the other completion dates were eighteen to twenty-four months. The early completion date was an important factor for us, as we didn't want to outstay our welcome with Nicola.

We went back to our hotel, and after our evening meal we reviewed the day's events. I was still reluctant to commit to the property that Bill had taken to, but we all agreed that it was the best value for money. Although it did not tick all the boxes, it did fulfil most of the things on my wish list. Frank and Sheila, along with Carole and Rob, and even Bill and May, were all thinking of the same house.

We decided to go and have a second look the next morning; we all got along together, and the fact that we would already know some of our neighbours when we finally moved out there was appealing.

The first row of houses on the development was completed, and we could see that already the people who had moved in had made improvements. Even the planting of shrubs and the different tiles had made a difference to the outside of the houses.

The three houses which we had reserved were in the last row to be completed and, after some discussion with the agent regarding what was included and what extras we needed, we all signed up. Bill and May would have the next house but one to us, and Frank and Sheila would be five houses away from us. But they were using their homes for holidays; we were the only ones who would be living there.

Afterwards, we were buzzing with excitement, and Lynne took us to a shop which supplied everything for a home. It was possible to get a package which virtually provided everything needed, but as we were bringing quite a lot of our own stuff out we only needed the electrical white goods. We also bought four single beds.

Bill and May bought quite a lot of things, as they would be starting from scratch – as would Frank and Sheila.

The rest of the trip was taken up with officialdom; we had to go to the bank to open an account, and sign up for utility services.

We rang Nicola and told her our news, but she wasn't over the moon, as she was worried that we had jumped in too quickly. We reassured her that we were very happy with the house.

We left Spain after exchanging phone numbers, etc with our soon-to-be neighbours, expecting to meet up again in a few months' time. We were to pay the money in stages over the next few months so that by the time we moved in the house would be paid for.

Back home with Nicola and Elliot, we began to plan for the big day. Bill and I went to any sale in the area, and bought anything and everything for the new house: kettle, toaster, electric ceiling fans for every room and even a fire surround and electric fire, as there was no central heating and we were told that it was quite chilly in winter, especially in the evenings.

We were told that we would get regular updates on the progress of the building, but we never did. We would ring the agents in England, but would be continually fobbed off. We kept sending the payments as and when they were due, but couldn't find out just when the house would be ready. We phoned Spain and were told that the building program was running late.

As we hadn't a clue as to exactly when the house would be ready, we decided to move back up to Yorkshire. Martin had moved in with his girlfriend, but still paid the rent on the house that he had, so we decided to move into that place for the rest of our stay in England. Just before we moved back, Martin and his girlfriend, Lyn, came to see us. I thought that they had just come down to do some Christmas shopping in London, but they produced a little picture – a scan. Martin was going to be a dad! He was forty-four and I never thought that he would be a dad. We were very surprised and delighted.

Once we were back in Yorkshire, we tried to find out something – or anything – about the progress in Spain. It was very worrying, as we were sending all this money to goodness knows where and we were hearing some real horror stories from different sources. We were in touch with Frank, and he told us that he was going out to Spain in March and wasn't coming home until he got some answers.

We did feel better after that, as we knew that one way or

Diamonds in the Coal Dust

another we would get a better picture. Two weeks later, we received a letter from Frank and, better still, a photograph of the site of our house. The footings were in – hooray – apparently there had been a problem with the labour force, but at least there was some action at last. Frank said his house wasn't started yet, as they were working their way down the street and Frank's house would be one of the last to be finished. It was obvious though that it wouldn't be ready on schedule. We were slightly reassured by Frank's reporting, but were still getting a little impatient at the lack of urgency from the agent and the builder.

The house we were staying in was far from ideal, but we were grateful just to have somewhere to stay without involving anyone else, so we just had to bite the bullet and sit it out.

During one of Bill's heated monthly phone calls, the agent snapped at him, 'It's not even started yet!' That did it.

'Right,' he said. 'We're off to Spain to kick ass.'

A few days later, we were on our way, prepared for the worst. We had booked into a hotel, and after refreshments we set off in our hire car to check out the building site. We couldn't believe how much building activity was going on in the area. As we turned into our development, we couldn't believe our eyes – to the side of the road where our houses sat, which had been waste ground a few months before, there stood row upon row of new houses, all completed. Obviously they had a better builder than we had. But the most exciting thing for us was the sight of the row of houses in our development. The first four were completed, then came ours and the one next to us, which were both built up to the roof. Bill and May's had not been started, nor had Frank and Sheila's, but the footings were there. Bill took photographs of me standing on what would eventually be our patio, and also photos of Frank's. I think we were so relieved that so much progress had been made when we had stopped expecting it that we felt positively euphoric.

We walked around the rest of the houses, where they had been completed, and it was surprising what a difference a few tiles made to the outside of the house. Some of the owners had put wrought-iron railings around. There were lots of additions, all helping to improve the starkness of the outside, which was one of the factors which had deterred me from buying in the first place. Bill couldn't wait to put his stamp on our house, but it would be some little time yet, I was sure. The occupants of one of the houses invited us in to see the final appearance after it was dressed up. It looked lovely, even better than the show house.

After satisfying ourselves that our money hadn't been hijacked, we enjoyed the rest of our stay. We returned home with light hearts, and things got even better when our fourth grandchild was born. Ellie was beautiful, like a little doll, and dark like her mum. Martin was so proud of her, and I was glad that she was born before we left for Spain.

Nicola was settled into her new house and was enjoying her job, although I think she found it a bit demanding. Elliot was awarded a place at Guildford Grammar School, which had a very good reputation. He loved it and soon made friends there.

We had been given another completion date for our house; this time it was for the end of September, and as that was only a couple of months ahead, we were quite pleased. We got a letter to tell us that Sheila was not well and was going into hospital for an operation. That put things into perspective for them. We sent word, hoping that she would soon be back to A1 condition.

Maria's house had been completed, so they had sold up and were over in Spain already. They phoned us up now and again, and we told them that it wouldn't be long before we were joining them there.

The good thing about renting the house we were in was that it was in the village where Bill had been born, where I had worked for many years and where Martin and his family lived, so we were able to keep in touch with many of our friends. Bill did have the odd day fishing, but most of his stuff was packed away ready for the move. I had the odd day out with my friends, especially Flo. She had shown an interest in the brochures which I had looked at with her, and she intimated that she might join us once we were established, perhaps in a house quite near to ours.

Martin and Lyn arranged to have Ellie christened before we left. It was a nice get-together for all the family. My Hollie was godmother and she was very proud. Ellie was an angel.

Diamonds in the Coal Dust

September came and went with no completion date forthcoming. It was very frustrating, as we couldn't book a carrier for the things we were taking with us, or book our flights. We had bought so much stuff, including new bed linen and towels to match the tiles in the bathrooms. We weren't taking TVs, as we weren't sure whether they would work out there.

We finally got the phone call in November – we would be leaving in two weeks' time, and were booked into a hotel for four days, to give us a chance to sign the deeds and make the final payment. That would entail a trip to the notary. We also had to arrange for the things we had purchased in Spain to be delivered. The rep would be running us about until we actually got the keys.

It was all systems go; we had to contact the carrier to collect our stuff so that it would be on its way as soon as us.

We rang Frank and Sheila; she was recovering at home after her operation. They hadn't heard anything about their house, and neither had Bill and May. But once we were there we could keep them wised up with progress.

It was exciting, and not too sad, as we were only a couple of hours away – hardly the same as when we went to Australia. We knew also that we could look forward to plenty of visitors.

We had a family night out before we left; Nicola and Elliot and her friend came, and Ann and her girls, and also Martin and Lyn with Ellie. Unfortunately Lyn had to take Ellie home a little early because she became a little fractious, but it was a lovely night.

Bill left the old car for Martin to dispose of as he saw fit, and he drove us to the airport in his car. When we arrived in Alicante, the rep picked us up and took us to our hotel. We were to be picked up the next morning to deal with the monetary side of things; it was going to be no holiday for the next few days.

Bill rang the carrier in England and gave them the details of our property and also his mobile number. It would be some time before we had a landline.

We had taken sleeping bags with us in our luggage, as we expected to be camping out in the house until our things came from England. Going to the notary was an experience. There was no obvious pecking order, just a crowd like at a football match, all milling about in one big room. Some people were sitting on the floor, but most were standing, quite patiently actually, just waiting for their particular rep to come and tell them when it was their turn. How on earth anybody made sense of the appointments system was beyond me. Things did get done eventually, but by the time we got out it was too late for the rep to take us to our property. So we had to spend another night in the hotel; we were far from happy but, after the wait we had had, what was one more night?

Bill rang the carrier and they said that they were already on their way, and would give him a ring the next day. We were very surprised, as we hadn't expected our stuff for a couple of weeks. Probably we were remembering our experience in Australia.

We were up bright and early the next morning and so was the rep; at 9 a.m. sharp we were off to our new home. The weather was atrocious, and the unmade road was just a sea of red mud. It was a good job we didn't have carpets down.

We let ourselves in and almost immediately two workmen turned up to replace the patio door, as someone had nicked the original one. They were closely followed by the men who were delivering our white goods and the beds we had bought some months earlier. A cleaner also came, to ask whether everything was OK, and on checking we had to tell him that the upstairs toilet had been used and not flushed. No problem – he gave both bathrooms a good going-over. In the meantime, the furniture men had built up the four beds, and set to work installing the cooker, washing machine and the fridge-freezer. We couldn't fault the team; they were very efficient and helpful.

The house was better than we remembered, and we were feeling quite excited about it, even though it was bucketing down outside.

We decided to go for a walk to get our bearings, and to find a shop where we could get something to eat. On the way back, Bill's mobile rang. It was the hauliers letting him know that they would be with us in a couple of hours. That was great news, as we had been expecting to sleep in sleeping bags that night. Things were looking better all the time.

Diamonds in the Coal Dust

It was very cold in the house, and we sat huddled on our cases, but not for long. Bill's phone rang again and it was the delivery men wanting directions for our house – they were out on the main road leading to our development. Bill told them to stay where they were and he would go to them and direct them back to us. It wasn't easy, as it was pitch black. It wasn't too long before they all turned up, though, and they immediately began unloading all our things.

Bill asked them to stack the boxes up in the lounge, and we would sort everything out; after all, we had plenty of time. We were the only ones in the street. The boxes and packages stretched from the stairs to the door, but it only took them a good hour to unload everything. Bill offered them a bottle of beer – we couldn't make them a cup of tea – and they were very grateful, though eager to get on their way. I think they were going for a drink and not setting off back to England until the next day, taking another load home with them.

We closed the door after them and just looked at each other. Where did we start? We decided to unpack two boxes at a time, starting with the crockery and the kettle, so that we could at least have a cup of tea as and when we wanted one. After a drink, we were ready for the off. Bill said that he was going to start with the fire as it was so cold. We had a little contretemps, as Bill and I couldn't agree where to put the fire; unusually I got my own way, and afterwards Bill did agree that I was right. Once the fire surround was in place and the fire installed, it straight away felt cosier. I unpacked the duvets and the bed linen so at least we could have a good night's sleep.

The schedule which we had set ourselves came and went; we just kept unpacking and having a drink and then unpacking some more. Our double bed was erected, the grandfather clock put in place, and the dining table and chairs were settled on their spots. I am not sure what time it was when we knocked off, but it was very late. Not that it mattered, as we had nothing better to do.

By the next afternoon, we even had ornaments in place. There were no light fittings, just wires hanging from the ceilings, but the day before Bill had been to the *ferreteria*, which sold everything you could possibly need to fix up your home. He bought a holder which he screwed the wires into, and then put an electric light bulb into the holder. It served very well as an emergency measure. We couldn't believe that there weren't even light sockets in any of the rooms. We had brought electric fans with a three-light built in with them, and one by one Bill installed them in every room. It took time, and I had to help him, as he couldn't hold the fans and screw them up at the same time. There was a little bit of cursing, but not much.

It was obvious that we were going to need transport, so Bill went to the local car dealer. He had quite a selection of cars, some better than others, and we ended up buying an Escort, quite a tidy little car. Now that we were mobile, everything seemed much easier. After two days of unpacking, we went for a ride to see Maria and Norman. They looked very comfortable in their house, but I liked the layout of our house much more.

It was only two weeks to Christmas, but we wouldn't be putting the tree or any decorations up this year.

After we had been in the house for a few days, I was laid in bed one morning and I noticed a dark patch on the bedroom wall. The next morning, it had moved further up the wall. Bill went to fetch the building site foreman who was working on the rest of the houses further down the street, which weren't yet completed. He took one look at it and said, 'Big problem.'

Yes, we wanted to know that. He went off and came back with two workmen, who proceeded to knock a big hole through the bedroom wall into the bathroom. I was horrified. Bill watched what they were doing and realised that there had been a leak in the pipes, which were behind the tiles in the bathroom. They didn't seem at all alarmed that we had a gaping hole in the bedroom wall, and it was now open plan with the bathroom. However, within two more days you couldn't even see where the leak had been, and the tiles in the bathroom had been replaced.

The week before Christmas was very quiet, even desolate. The people who had already moved in seemed to have gone back home for the holidays. Maria and Norman invited us to their house for lunch on Boxing Day, and for Christmas dinner, I bought a chicken from the supermarket, but was horrified to find that the head and feet were still on it. Not a good start, but I persevered and we had some sort of Christmas lunch. I actually took a photograph of Bill sitting at the table, eating his dinner and with a glass of wine. It looked so sad, but we wouldn't have another Christmas dinner quite as desolate as that. We never had another Christmas alone.

After dinner, we went for a walk; it was quite pleasant – at least it had stopped raining. We walked along the seafront and came across a group of Germans walking along and laughing together, all with Santa Claus hats on... that made us smile.

On Boxing Day, we had a lovely Christmas dinner with Maria and Norman, and then Norman took us for a ride to a warehouse to look at suites, as we had nothing comfortable to sit on. We came away having bought two settees, which we would get in two or three weeks' time. Back at Maria's, it was lovely to sit in comfort and also to watch television, which we had missed, especially at Christmas. They were having the whole of their patio area tiled and it looked super. An English neighbour of theirs was doing it, and apparently he did it for a living, so Bill asked Maria to find out whether he would be willing to do ours. She said he had a backlog of work, but that she would ask him for us. She actually phoned him while we were there and he said he was booked up for two months, but promised that he would get back to us when he was able. It would be good to walk on tiles, instead of ploughing through mud.

In January, we met our next-door neighbours, Tony and Sandra. They lived in the south of England, in fact quite close to Nicola. The house in Spain was a holiday home for them, and they intended to come out for a fortnight every six weeks. Bill and Tony hit it off straightaway, and we were to spend many happy hours together.

As the houses further down the street were completed, Frank turned up to finalise things with his property, but Sheila was still not well enough to travel. The weather had turned grim again and when Frank said that he had to go to the solicitor at the same time as his furniture was due, Bill offered to keep an eye on things. When the delivery arrived, the men were wading backwards and forwards through the mud, carrying furniture in and out. Bill tried to lay cardboard down to catch most of the mess, but he didn't have much luck – it was a quagmire.

Maddy Worth

Frank arrived back shortly after the furniture men had departed and he soon set to mopping the mess up. I did feel sorry for him, but he didn't seem to mind too much.

His next-door neighbour, Margaret, invited him to have tea with them, and then he joined Bill on our patio for a few bevvies.

Bill had got into the habit of sitting on the patio in the evening with half a dozen bottles of beer. He smoked as well, but not in the house, so he would sit outside with his fag in one hand and the bottle in the other. Frank was not much of a beer drinker – he preferred a glass of wine – but when Bill had finished with him he was a beer drinker – at least, in Bill's company he was. One night, they had been enjoying one or two (or three of four), and Frank leaned over to reach another bottle. The plastic chairs that they were sitting on were only cheap things, and, as he leaned, one of the legs collapsed. He rolled over ever so gently, with one leg stuck through the balustrades. He was laughing so much that he couldn't get up, and we couldn't help him; he was like a beached whale. It wouldn't be the last time that one or the other of them was a little bit the worse for wear.

The houses directly opposite ours were of a different style to ours, and were gradually being taken over by their new owners. As with ours, they were mostly holiday homes. The one directly opposite us was bought by an elderly couple from Ireland. They came and introduced themselves as Pat and Joe. They were brilliant, especially Joe, who needed a good sense of humour to deal with Bill, who insisted on saying 'Top o' the mornin' to ye' – Joe would try to answer with a Yorkshire accent. Pat was quiet, not Irish herself, but she had lived there for many years since they were married.

We had been in Spain probably four months when Nicola, Peter and Elliot came to visit for the first time. Nicola had been offered a directorship at work, and was earning good money but working very hard. They were very impressed with the house, and we enjoyed showing them round Torrevieja and the surrounding area.

Bill and May had been out to their house to complete, but I don't think that they made much headway. Bill had no transport and he wouldn't hire a car. We had them over for a meal a couple

Diamonds in the Coal Dust

of times, but I got the feeling that May wasn't well. The house next door to them was owned by a retired doctor and his wife, but they hadn't been there long when the doctor's wife died, so eventually he sold up and went back home. The couple who bought their house were from down south, and were intending to spend a month in Spain and a month in England. Jean was a right laugh.

Gradually our little development was building up into a nice little community, and everybody seemed to get along with each other. Bill was sitting on the patio one morning when he noticed a couple, two houses up the street, sitting outside on their patio. He had never seen them before; we had understood that the house had not yet been sold. Bill walked up to have a word with them, and to ask if they were OK. They said that they had bought the house and were waiting for a delivery. An hour later, they were still sitting there, and Bill asked them to come to our house for a cup of tea and a sandwich. They were quite upset – at least, the lady was – and it turned out that they had bought the property, and the rep had just dropped them off. They had no electricity, no furniture and no transport – what a way to treat a customer. Bill was infuriated, and said that he would go into the electric box and connect them up himself. The rep was supposed to have arranged for their furniture to arrive. Bill insisted that Terry, who was the gentleman concerned, ring the agent and tell him to get himself back down there.

By this time, it was beginning to get dark. The agent turned up and got on the phone to the electricity company and the furniture firm. Bill told Terry and Maureen to go to one of the little cafés locally and get something to eat; he said that he would keep an eye out for the arrival of the furniture. In the meantime, he rigged up a cable from our house to theirs, and took two bedside lamps for them to use.

When the electrician finally came, Bill of course gave him the benefit of his knowledge in no uncertain terms. The electrician assured Bill that he hadn't know anything about it; obviously someone had slipped up somewhere.

That was one good thing about the Spanish, work didn't stop at 6 p.m. At 8 p.m., just as Maureen and Terry arrived back, the furniture turned up. It was 11 p.m. when the men left, as they had to assemble the beds and fix the light fittings – what an ordeal for them. But then everyone who bought a place in Spain had their own story to tell.

We became good friends with Maureen and Terry; they were a lovely couple, and deserved better than the treatment that they got, especially as Terry was not very well at the time.

On our street, there was a good mix of ex-pats from all over the UK. Frank and Sheila were from Wales, Bill and May from Scotland, Pat and Joe from Ireland and most of the rest were from down south. I wouldn't have thought that Bill would get on with everybody, or at least some of them, being a loud, bombastic, sometimes brash Yorkshire man, but he got on great with almost everybody. They were of the opinion that 'what you see is what you get'. He would do anything for anybody and not want anything in return.

He had every tool imaginable; if we went shopping, he would always make a beeline for the gadgets and tools. So if any of the men in the street were short of an implement, Bill would have it, and if he didn't do the job for them, he would certainly lend them the tool to do the job.

Things were quiet for most of the time, especially if it was a period when most of the holidaymakers were absent. So quiet, in fact, that the least little happening would turn out to be a major occasion. The day the road was tarmacked was a very exciting event – no more mud and dust everywhere! The second major event was the switching on of the street lights. The Blackpool illuminations did not cause more excitement than our street lights being turned on. Tony took a photograph and added the inscription, 'The day the lights were switched on'. How sad was that? The day we got the landline in for the telephone was very important; it meant that we were in regular contact with the family and the outside world.

Looking back, it does seem sad that these things were so important, but, believe me, they did take on major significance.

We had a swimming pool just for the use of our development, and very nice it was, too, but there were rules and regulations. By Spanish law, each urbanisation had to have a president and committee, and each street had a street warden. The president was supposed to see that the rules and regulations were adhered to. Anyone suspected of breaking the rules could be reported and issued with a warning. Every resident was given a copy of the rules, but problems arose when a resident had visitors on holiday, as they didn't see why they should be told what to do. The swimming pool gates had to be kept shut and locked so that children couldn't wander in, as they were only supposed to be in the pool under the supervision of an adult. Each resident had a key to the pool, but you would get bathers going in and propping the gates open, so that any Tom, Dick or little Harry could wander in. It was a safety thing. Sun beds and lilos were also banned, as apparently a child had drowned under a lilo. Of course, skinny-dipping was banned and also bathing after dark. You would think that most of these rules were obvious, but not to some know-all residents. Three or four of the full-time residents took it in turns to check the gates and make sure that they were locked before dark, putting a chain round the gate. Bill was our street warden and also took a turn on pool duty, keeping an eye on things and making sure that the rules were observed. This was not without its drawbacks, as you would get some mouthy residents muttering 'Hitler' or 'OK, boss' under their breath. But the rules were for the most part safety issues and made by the Spanish government.

We heard that Pat and Joe had let their property out for six months, to two ladies from England. I think that they had come to check the area out with a view to buying a property. One of them was a middle-aged lady and the other one was her daughter, who was probably in her mid-twenties. They had driven over from England with two dogs and a cat in a car full of possessions. Sheila – the mother – was a real lady, but Caroline I just couldn't work out – she seemed a bit bohemian. The house itself wasn't actually very suitable for two active dogs. One of them was a lovely spaniel and the other one was a pointer, which was very highly strung. The mum and daughter went out for a meal, leaving the dogs inside the house. The pointer was hurling herself at the door, making the most distressing noise. When the two of them came back, Bill told them about the dog, so the next time they went out, they left the dogs in the yard. The pointer escaped and it took myself and a chap who happened to be passing some time to catch her. It was quite upsetting, as she was so frightened.

A couple of weeks later, Bill and I were sitting in the lounge and I saw two ladies talking to Caroline. After they had gone, I could see that she was holding a small animal. I mentioned it to Bill and he told me to go and find out what the two ladies wanted. It transpired that the two ladies were Spanish, and had told Caroline that they had found this tiny dog wandering on some waste ground. She told them that she had already got two dogs, but they walked away and left her with it anyway, asking her to take it to the vet.

Caroline was a dog lover and felt sorry for the little fellow, but she did say, 'I can't possibly do with another dog.' Bill said that we would have him until the owner showed up – fat chance. Caroline offered to take me to her vet to find out whether he was microchipped – some chance of that as well.

I had never seen such a funny, pathetic-looking little dog in all my life. He was like a little piglet, with hardly any fur, pink eyes and nose and his claws were overgrown; they had obviously not been walked on enough to wear them down. He didn't even know how to climb steps – we had to carry him up and down until he got the hang of it. He was extremely timid, and wouldn't look you in the eye when you spoke to him; he would turn his head away from you – it was very distressing.

Caroline drove me to the vet while I held the little dog on my lap; he trembled violently the whole of the journey. The vet was lovely and told us that he didn't expect to find a microchip in him, as he said that the dog had been neglected and obviously abandoned. He thought that he was probably about twelve months old, but he couldn't be sure. He checked him over and clipped his claws, and also gave him a worming tablet, then asked whether we intended to keep him.

I said, 'Yes, if nobody claims him.' The vet suggested that if we still had him in four weeks' time, I should take him back and have him chipped and castrated.

I took him home and Bill called him Albi, short for albino, as

Diamonds in the Coal Dust

that was what he seemed to be. Bill went on the computer and made some flyers, advertising for the owners of a missing small dog to contact us, but, of course, nobody claimed him.

Albi and Bill became great mates, and the little dog eventually came out of his shell, but he was still quite timid. If you called for him, he would always come, but very slowly and almost crawling on his belly.

After a month of nobody claiming him, Bill and I took him back to the vet so that he could be chipped and also booked in for his operation for the following week. Each time we went to the vet's, the waiting room was full of mostly English people with their dogs, and they all had a story to tell.

Albi was never going to win any competitions with his looks; in fact, he was in the yard one day when a little boy went past with his dad; he saw Albi and asked his dad, 'Is that a guinea pig, Dad?' But he had a lovely nature, especially considering the life he must have endured previously. He loved everybody, other dogs included, and, as time went by, Bill would just have to pick up his walking stick and tap it on the tiled floor, and Albi would be there ready for the off – even if he appeared to be fast asleep, he would be up like a shot. Off the pair of them would go, Bill to do his rounds of the pool, and Albi just to tag along, sniffing every blade of grass. Sometimes Bill would come back on his own, if Albi had been diverted, but everybody knew Albi, as they did Bill. If any of our friends were out for a holiday, Albi knew, and would leave Bill and bob in to their houses to see if there was anything going. At Sheila and Frank's, he would walk in and sit outside the fridge, as Sheila used to give him cheese, which he loved. It was so embarrassing – Sheila would be sitting there in the lounge, and Albi would walk straight past her into the kitchen. At Tony and Sandra's, he would stand with his head poked through the balustrades, as Sandra would give him treats. He would spend most of the two weeks that they were there with his head between the rails.

After the six-month rental period for Caroline and Sheila was up, they decided to move on, and I must say that it was good to see Pat and Joe again. Bill gave Joe a drinking mug with the Tykes motto on it: 'Hear all, see all and say nowt; Eat all, sup all and pay

Maddy Worth

nowt; and if thy ever does owt for nowt, allus do it for thissen.' Bill told Joe that he had to learn it before he came out to Spain again.

Every year, on St Patrick's Day, Pat and Joe would go to the Irish Bar. Joe would have a couple of glasses of Guinness and buy three hats, one for himself, one for Bill and one for Tony. Each year, they were a different design; one year they were bright green with orange hair, a bit like a leprechaun's, and one year they were black and white, like a glass of Guinness. I always took photographs of the three of them with these silly hats on; it was a kind of ritual.

Bill loved all things Irish. He had nearly all the Foster and Allen tapes, and knew the words to most of them – his favourite was *Maggie* – and he would play his tapes and sing along loudly.

As I mentioned earlier, he had bought himself a bicycle before we moved out to Spain, as he couldn't walk far because of his bad back. He thought that the bike would be good exercise for him. Albi didn't mind at all running behind the bike. Joe had a bad hip, and he also found it difficult walking very far. Bill spotted an old bicycle at the side of the bins that someone had chucked out, so he wheeled it home and he and Joe set about making it roadworthy. It wasn't too long before Joe was getting about on two wheels; it made life a lot easier for him.

Every year after the first one, Nicola came out to us for the Christmas holiday, and I really looked forward to it. Elliot and Peter also came, and they would always bring the video camera. On Christmas morning, we would open our presents and it would be captured on camera. Bill looked forward more nowadays to the present-opening ceremony, and Nicola always had a joke present for her dad. One year, she gave him an instruction booklet on how to play a didgeridoo. He looked at it blankly, but then it was followed up by a large parcel containing a didgeridoo – a genuine one from Australia. He was thrilled to bits, and even managed to make some weird and wonderful noises with it.

Another year, she gave him a DVD wrapped up.

'That's no good to me,' he said.

Diamonds in the Coal Dust

Nicola asked him why not, and of course he told her that he didn't own a DVD player.

'Oh, well, you had better open this parcel then.' Of course, it contained a new DVD player.

The third surprise was the best; the first parcel contained a musical instrument instruction book. When he opened his big present, it was an accordion; he loved that.

When he first started playing it, Albi would sit and howl, but he would go into the bedroom, take Albi with him and shut the door and practise. Bill was very musical; he could play anything he got his hands on, and it wasn't long before he was playing all his Foster and Allen favourites. Albi quickly got used to hearing it, and would happily lie on the floor and listen with his eyes closed.

We always looked forward to Sandra and Tony coming out, and, when they were due, I would get them milk and salad and a French stick, and probably a pizza, as it would usually be late in the evening when they arrived. Although they came every six weeks, we always seemed to have plenty to talk about. We would usually go out for a meal at least once during their stay, and they would come to us, and we would go to them; of course, there would be plenty of the old vino flowing.

Sheila and Frank also came out at regular intervals, but not as often as Tony and Sandra. Bill and May didn't come out very often at all, as Bill had a hotel in Scotland, so it was difficult for him to pick a suitable time to leave the business. It was a shame that they weren't getting the benefit of their house.

After Frank and Sheila's house came Margaret and David's. He was a farmer, so they couldn't spend as much time there as she would have liked, but sometimes she came on her own. One New Year's Eve, we had a party with quite a few people and quite a lot of booze. David was a big man, even bigger than Bill, and the pair of them were still going long after everyone else had left. When the time came for Margaret and David to go home, we couldn't get him up off the settee. With a determined effort, the three of us managed to haul him up, and we watched as Margaret very slowly walked him from our house to theirs.

On the other side of Margaret were Charlie and Iris, and their Doberman dog, Mollie. Iris didn't get out much; if fact, she never went walking at all. Charlie would take her in the car every day to a little bar, where she would sit outside with Mollie and have a drink or two while Charlie went to the bookies nearby. I think that she was an alcoholic. She had a pretty face, but didn't have a pennyworth of meat on her bones.

Martin and Lyn came out to see us for the first time, and they loved it. Bill let them have the use of our car so they were able to explore the area a bit. Ellie was nearly three when they brought her for the second time; we went into Torrevieja one Sunday to walk along the seafront. There were crowds of people, mostly Spanish, as that was what Spanish people did on Sunday afternoons. It was a lovely sunny day and the street people were out, all doing their own thing to earn a bob. One young woman was dressed as Minnie Mouse. It made Ellie's day – she kept running up to Minnie and flinging her arms round her, and we couldn't prise her away. We sat on the seafront, having a coffee at one of the bars and we hadn't noticed that Minnie had moved up the front towards us. Ellie spotted her and set off, running towards her. I thought that Minnie was going to turn around and run away, but she didn't and Ellie had her in a bear hug, saying, 'I love you, Minnie.' We decided to move on with Ellie still shouting, 'I love you, Minnie!' It was so funny.

Albi loved it when any of the family came, and after they had gone home and we had the house to ourselves again, he would mope about for days.

One afternoon, Bill and I had gone for a ride in the car and parked up to sit and watch the sea roll in. When Bill opened the car door, he noticed a plastic carrier bag down by the side of the car. He looked inside it and found an assortment of plants; they looked as though they had been pulled up from a garden and thrown out. Neither of us recognised what they were, but Bill took them home and stuck them in the bit of garden that we had, which at most was a thirty-inch strip around the edge of the patio. We had bougainvillea, plumbago and an assortment of bits and pieces.

Not too long afterwards, the newly planted greenery put in an appearance: they grew to beautiful, tall, stately, cream calla lilies. Everyone came to admire them, and as one died, it would be

Diamonds in the Coal Dust

replaced by several others. Bill was so proud of them, and rightly so. We were asked whether we could take cuttings from them for people, but they grew so far down into the hard ground that it was almost impossible to get at the roots.

We had news from home that Martin and Lyn were expecting their second baby, and I arranged to go back home so that I could be with Ellie if things began to move during the night.

I had been back to England several times since we had moved to Spain. I liked to look up old friends and see the grandchildren. Sometimes I would just go for a week, but sometimes it would be for a fortnight. I always tried to get Bill three warm, fresh pork pies from the local butcher. I would call for them on the way to the airport before flying home. I think that Bill was more pleased to get the pork pies than to see me home!

I was due to stay for two weeks for the birth of the baby, but after ten days there was no sign of anything happening. On the eleventh night, Martin came into my bedroom to tell me that they were on their way to the hospital.

I got up with Ellie the next morning and told her that Mummy and Daddy had gone to get the baby, and she didn't seem too concerned. At lunchtime, Martin came home and said that they had had a little boy. In the afternoon, Martin took Ellie and me to see the new baby; she couldn't understand why Mummy and her little brother were not coming home with us. They came home the next day, two days before I was to return home.

I rang Bill and told him the news. He was thrilled that it was a boy, who would take his surname through to another generation. Lewis was a gorgeous baby and very well behaved, and Ellie loved him to bits. It was a shame that I was leaving so soon, but I knew that it wouldn't be long before I saw them all again. Martin took me to the airport for my trip home – with Bill's pork pies, of course. I loved flying; it didn't bother me one bit travelling on my own.

Bill had never been back to England since we left, but he had booked a flight for three months' time, as he wanted to renew his driving licence. I had renewed mine when I was in England, but as the new licences carried a photograph, Bill had to apply in person for his.

Bill met me at the airport gate as he always did, and as I came through the gate, I spotted him. I thought to myself that he didn't look well. Although I always filled the freezer with food before I came away, usually most of it was still untouched when I arrived back home. He always told me that he had eaten out for most of the time.

'You look tired,' I said to him.

'I'm OK,' he said.

Sure enough, when I looked in the freezer, all the food was still there. Bill did brighten up when I told him about the baby and Ellie, and even said that he was glad to see me home.

Tony and Sandra came out for their visit, so we did the socialising bit. We went to our favourite restaurant with them and we also had them for a meal. We always enjoyed their company, and Albi was always pleased to see them as well.

I would always offer to help Sandra with the washing up after the meal, but she always insisted that she and Tony would do it after we left. A bit like when they came to ours for a meal – Sandra always offered to give a hand with the pots, and I would say, 'No, it's OK, Bill will help me with them after you've gone.' Two minutes after they had left, Bill would have a bottle of beer in each hand and I would be up to my elbows in suds. I suppose he had to keep his beer arm exercised to keep it in trim.

Before we had been in Spain too long, Bill found himself a watering hole, not too far from where we lived, which he supported with great enthusiasm, to the tune of two or three nights a week. It was called 'Paolo's' and Bill said that it was a great little business, but I think sometimes he was the only customer there. Paolo extended the place and started serving food, but I don't think that it took off. One night, Bill persuaded Tony and Sandra and Frank and Sheila and me to go for a meal. It was dire. I felt sorry for Bill, as he had recommended it. It didn't stop Bill from going there, and he loyally continued to give them his custom to the tune of a few pints per night. Fortunately, the car knew the way home by itself, and it always brought him home safely.

Probably once a fortnight we would drive to a little Spanish town called Pilar de Horadada, about fifteen minutes' drive up the road

Diamonds in the Coal Dust

– not for anything in particular, just to pass a morning and potter around the 100-*peseta* shops. Sometimes Bill would say, 'I will stay in the car while you have a look around.' It all depended on how good or bad his back was. This particular day, he decided to come with me, as I think that there was some tool or other that he needed. He always parked in the same place, quite close to one of the bigger shops, which was like Aladdin's cave. He walked round all the shops with me and then suggested that we go for a coffee to his favourite coffee shop. It was a Spanish bar, but the girl who usually served was Russian. Everybody was very friendly.

We came home and I made a sandwich for lunch. Bill complained that his back was hurting quite a lot. I thought he had probably done too much walking, and gave him a couple of his tablets. He lay on the sofa but couldn't get comfortable. By around 4 p.m. he was obviously in considerable discomfort, and he asked me to get the doctor for him. I thought he believed he was back home – I hadn't a clue how to get the doctor to him.

As it happened, the only friends of ours who were about were Jean and Fred, who lived two houses down from us. I asked Fred what he thought I should do, and he offered to take me to the clinic. When we arrived there it was out of hours, so of course nobody was supposed to be ill. The receptionist called for a doctor and a Mohammed something-or-other came to the desk. I explained to him that my husband was very ill and asked whether the doctor could visit him. The answer was very brief.

'*Non*,' he said, 'he come here.'

I told him that my husband could not walk, and his answer was to write a telephone number down, give it to me and say, 'You ring that.'

We rushed back home, and I phoned the number and requested transport for my husband. The voice at the other end of the phone kept repeating '*Non comprende*.' I used my little bit of Spanish to ask for emergency transport, but the answer was the same: '*Non comprende*.'

By this time, Bill was rolling around in agony, saying that he couldn't stand it any longer. Fred helped me to get him into the car and we drove to the clinic. We somehow managed to get him there, out of the car and into the surgery, with much strong language. The doctor stood looking at him while I tried to explain the problem.

Bill kept on saying, 'It's my back, it's my back.'

The doctor never examined him, just gave me a sample bottle and said, 'Urine.'

I took Bill to the toilet and got a specimen; he then went and lay across three chairs in the waiting room.

The doctor gave the sample to a nurse, who took it away with her, bringing it back five minutes later, saying, 'Urine infection.' The doctor wrote a prescription and we got Bill into the car, picked up the tablets from the pharmacy and took him home.

I was very worried about him and was very grateful to Fred for his support. Bill went upstairs and lay on one of the beds, and I put the fan on him as it was so hot, then made him a drink and gave him his first lot of tablets. He couldn't get comfortable and sat on the edge of the bed. I suggested that I ran him a bath, as he could probably get comfortable in there.

He crawled out of the bath and into the bedroom, again sitting on the edge of the bed. I asked him if he wanted to lie down, but he said that he had got comfortable like that. I thought that the tablets had started to kick in. He actually nodded off to sleep sitting on the side of the bed. By this time, it was 10 p.m.

I went downstairs and let the dog have a little walk and made a cup of tea. I took it upstairs and stood looking at Bill. He had laid down and fallen asleep. I was so pleased; he seemed to be comfortable at last. At 12.30 a.m. I went in to him and told him that I was going to bed in the next room and to call me if he wanted anything. He didn't answer, so I thought he must still be asleep. I left all the lights on in case he woke up and wondered where he was. I was reading, but must have fallen asleep and woke up when I heard Bill call to me. It was 2.40 a.m. I dashed into his room and he said, 'Arm-leg.' He had obviously had a stroke, as he couldn't move one side, and his face was still on one side. I flew downstairs and phoned for an emergency ambulance. I asked for an English-speaking operator; a very nice lady came on the phone and I explained that my husband had suffered a stroke. She asked where we lived and told me to stay on the phone so that she could talk to the ambulance drivers and me at the same

Diamonds in the Coal Dust

time. None of the new developments had street signs and none of the emergency services knew one street from another.

She kept asking me for landmarks for them to recognise. I could hear Bill calling for me, so I told the lady I had to go to my husband – but she said that I couldn't leave the phone or they wouldn't have any contact with me and they would never find me.

Just then she said, 'They are at the mini roundabout, can someone come to meet them as they don't know where to go.' Who on earth was there at 2.55 a.m. except me? I scooped the dog up under my arm and ran out, leaving the door wide open. I ran down the street and could just see the blue flashing light on the ambulance. I was out of breath and was just hoping that the ambulance would see me before it set off. I was waving my arms about, and eventually they spotted me and began to come towards me. They caught up with me at the end of our street and slowly drove up behind me. I pointed upstairs and off they went. I followed them and found that they were looking down at Bill.

'Do something,' I said to them. They pushed me out of the bedroom, and – in that terrible moment – I knew he had gone.

One of them came downstairs and went to the ambulance for a respirator, but it was all too late. How could somebody with a water infection be dead a few hours later?

I sat frozen on the settee with Albi huddled beside me; I was very scared. After ten minutes or so, they came downstairs and one of them said, 'I'm sorry.' The other one was on the telephone, gabbling away in Spanish; then they both went out to the ambulance.

I went upstairs to Bill. They had lifted him off the bed and he was laid on the floor. He didn't look any different, just as though he were asleep. I left him there and went back downstairs. The ambulance men came back in and asked me several questions. Just then, a policeman arrived and the doctor, who spoke to the ambulance men; they left and two more young men came in who were in uniform. They asked me whether I would like a cup of tea; I thought that was strange, asking me if I wanted a drink in my own house. They kept trying to attract Albi's attention, but he didn't want to know. Somehow, with that wonderful animal awareness that they seem to have, Albi knew that everything was not OK. He didn't bark once at the assortment of people who came and went that awful night, he just followed their every move with his eyes, without leaving my side.

The next arrival was the young lady from the funeral parlour. She came with another gentleman and, when they arrived, the two young chaps left. Paqui, the young lady, sat down beside me and started to ask me about the burial. She was very nice and as sensitive as she could be under the circumstances. I had to make some decisions immediately, but I told her that my children would be out quite quickly, so she agreed to come the next afternoon. Two more men appeared, and Paqui said that they were going to take my husband away.

'Am I coming?' I asked her.

'No,' she said.

'Where am I going?' I asked her.

'You are staying here,' she said.

They carried Bill out, and Paqui followed, and then they were all gone. I went outside and it was very quiet and still. I felt like shouting out loud, 'Does anybody know what has happened in here?'

I went back into the house and wondered whether I had been dreaming, then I heard a sound upstairs. 'There', I thought, 'he is still there.' I ran upstairs and there was nobody there – just the crumpled sheets where Bill had laid just a short time before.

I looked at Albi and he looked at me, and I felt very sorry for myself.

It was 4.45 a.m. and obviously I couldn't ring the kids at that time of morning. It was an unreal feeling. It reminded me of the morning that Martin was born – how strange it was that one minute there were two people in our family and then there were three. But this time, one was gone and now there was only me.

I went upstairs and stripped the bedding from the four beds, came down and took the bedding off the bed downstairs, and put the washing machine on. Why did I do it? The sheets were clean – but I had nothing else to do. Then I got out the mop bucket and washed all the floors throughout the house. Each time the washing machine finished, in went another load until it was all done.

Diamonds in the Coal Dust

At 7 a.m. I began the awful job of ringing my kids. I knew they would all be up for work, and wanted to catch them before they set out. I can't imagine how terrible it must have been to have got that phone call at 7 a.m. Three times I had to do it, but what more could I say, just get those terrible four words out: 'Your dad has died.'

I rang Martin first, and he recognised my voice and answered quite chirpily; I said what I had to say – what more was there? – and then told him that I had to ring the girls, and I would talk to him later. Next came Nicola, and of course she was distraught. It didn't help that I had to say that I had to ring Ann, as I needed them all to know before I went into lengthy details. Nicola promised to ring me back, as did the other two, but I felt that they had to have a little time to absorb it all.

When I had finished the phone calls, I sat down and looked around; it was a nightmare. I took Albi for his walk before most people were knocking about, as I didn't feel like facing anyone at that time.

I kept looking out for Fred to appear on his patio, as he did at about 9 a.m. for a smoke. He finally appeared and rather than shout at him, I phoned. When he answered the phone, I just said, 'Fred, Bill has gone.'

Of course, he asked, 'Gone where?'

'He has died,' I managed to get out.

Fred shouted to Jean, and they both came running in.

'Where is he, is he upstairs?' Fred asked.

I had to tell him that Bill was gone. They were both put out that I hadn't called them at 3 a.m.

'But what could you have done?' I asked them.

'We could have been there for you,' said Jean. It was a relief to have someone to talk to, I must admit.

I told them of the evening's proceedings, and like me they couldn't believe it. They told me that I should not have been on my own, but ever since I was small, if I was hurting, I just wanted to be by myself and lick my wounds; I didn't like anyone to fuss around me.

As word got around, there was a steady stream of people to see me and offer their condolences. Everyone was so shocked – Bill

Maddy Worth

was a larger-than-life character, and he had never been in hospital in his life. I thought, and I am sure so did he, that he would live for ever.

Martin rang me to say he had got a flight and would be arriving at lunchtime. Fred said that he would go to the airport and pick him up. Nicola and Ann were arriving on separate flights that evening, so Martin and I would pick them up in Bill's car.

Pat and Joe had friends a few miles down the road, and they came on behalf of Pat and Joe to offer their condolences. It was unbelievable how the news had got around, as the only ones I had told were Fred and Jean. I had to make several phone calls back home to members of Bill's family.

Martin came just after lunchtime, and we hugged and cried, and cried and hugged, and tried to make sense of it but couldn't.

Paqui came again in the afternoon, and we decided that we would have Bill cremated and then, a little later, his ashes taken back to England for a memorial service. In Spain, burials are not in the ground, but put in holes in the wall, with a plaque and a picture on the end for relatives to visit. I always said to Bill, 'Don't put me in a hole in the wall. I want to be buried in England.'

But he always said, 'I don't care what you do with me – you can put me in the dustbin for all I care.'

The cremation service was to be the next day, as was the custom in Spain. We were to have a short service. Nicola was going to bring the latest Foster and Allen tape so that we could play 'Maggie' for him.

I rang Norman and Maria, and of course they were as shocked as everyone else. They said that they would be at the service.

I can't remember having anything to eat that day, and when we went to pick the girls up that night at the airport, I thought to have something to eat on the way back. In the event, we never did have anything to eat, as we were just too emotionally drained to think about food. In fact, we sat up most of the night just talking.

One strange thing did occur, though. Bill was fanatical about keeping the petrol in the tank of the car no lower than a quarter full – it just didn't happen. But when Martin drove the car to the airport, he noticed that the needle was on empty – in fact, we were worried that we wouldn't make it to a filling station. This

Diamonds in the Coal Dust

did make us wonder whether perhaps Bill had not been totally on the ball the day before when we went to Pilar de Horadada. Was it only the day before? I couldn't believe it.

The day of the cremation was very strange; it didn't have any structure, and we just drifted about, waiting until it was time to set off. When we arrived at the crematorium, I was surprised at how many people were there. Even the priest said that it was good to see so many people there; with most ex-pats, they did not have a big turnout, as most friends and family didn't have the time to get out there.

The service was sad for us, but it seemed to be a bit sterile compared to the one we might have had back home. Afterwards, most of the people who attended the service came back to the house with us. Bill would have been proud at how much beer was drunk to toast him. Most people had a tale to tell about Bill, most of them comical. Eventually everyone drifted away, and I suggested to my children that we go for a walk and have something to eat. Martin said, 'Why don't we call in at Paolo's and have a drink for my dad, then go for a meal?' We all thought it was a good idea, and off we went.

In Paolo's, there was only the lady who served behind the bar and I asked her whether Paolo was in. She said that he was at home, which was nearby. We decided to have a drink anyway, and were just about ready to leave, when Paolo walked in – I think that the barmaid must have phoned him. We explained to him that Bill had passed away and that we were having a drink for him. Paolo was really upset, and said that Bill had been in on the Sunday and had been fine. He explained to the barmaid, who didn't understand much English, and she was also upset. We all raised a glass to Bill and left to go to the restaurant.

We sat at a table outside an Italian restaurant and had a lovely meal. It was all spoilt for me when the music, which had been playing quietly in the background, suddenly brought it all back to me. It was Italian music, but the song that was being played was 'Oh My Beloved Father'. Much as I tried to swallow and not cry, I couldn't. Nicola asked what the matter was, and if someone had upset me, but I couldn't say. The children didn't recognise the tune, so there was no point in explaining to them and upsetting them also.

I think that we did sleep that night. The next day, Nicola set about sorting out paperwork on the computer. When she switched the machine on, there was an email from one of our neighbours; she wanted to know how things were. Most of our neighbours kept in touch by email when they were in England.

Nicola and I drew up a letter explaining what had happened, and she sent it off to as many of our friends as possible.

I was one of the first pupils at the school of hard knocks, and had bounced back more times than I cared to remember, but I was struggling. I dreaded the time when all the kids would have gone back home. Parts of my brain seemed to be going off in different directions, and I felt as if I should reach out and gather the errant pieces of my brain and put them back in the right places. My lovely kids kept me sane; they rallied around and supported me even when things weren't easy for themselves.

Jean and Fred were the only ones of our friends who were in Spain at that time, and I don't know what I would have done without them. One of our friends, who had received the email from us, rang me. Terry was very upset, as he had spoken to Bill a few days before. Maureen had phoned me to tell me when they were coming out and Bill had asked Maureen if he could speak to Terry. When Terry came on the phone, Bill said to him, 'Do me a favour, Terry, don't bother coming – it's much better without you.'

Terry called Bill a miserable old bugger and said that he was only coming out to make life hard for him. They both had a laugh about that, but Terry was upset that the last time they had spoken a few days earlier, Bill had been in such good spirits.

Ann went home two days later, and we all took her to the airport. She wasn't looking forward to the flight, as she didn't like travelling alone. Martin went home the next day; his baby was only a few weeks old and he had had to abandon Lyn, Ellie and Lewis to come to Spain. I did appreciate his support, though. Nicola was staying on another week, which I was very grateful for. I found it hard going to places that I had gone to regularly with Bill and having people ask, 'Where is he?' We would go to the local Chinese restaurant at least once a week, and the staff were very friendly. The first time I went with my daughter, the little girl who served us came up and said, 'Ah, no dad.' I had to explain that he wouldn't be coming any more. She was genuinely upset, and went to tell the other members of staff. I felt like walking around with a placard round my neck saying, 'I am on my own – my husband has died.'

Paqui brought Bill's ashes and also a big bill for the cremation, which I paid. She had put the urn in a carrying bag, as I had explained that I would be taking it back to England on the plane with me. She also gave me a covering letter in case they questioned it at the check-in.

Nicola and I drafted an Order of Service for the memorial service and decided which readings and songs would be suitable. I was hoping that the service could be arranged for a month ahead. We sorted through photographs of Bill and chose a fairly recent one, taken in happier times on a visit to Javea with Nicola and Elliot. Nicola would design and print the Order of Service cards when she went back home. She was going to organise it from her end, as it was very frustrating trying to liaise with different organisations from Spain on the telephone.

I was very sad to say goodbye to Nicola when she went home; it suddenly hit me that I was on my own – well, apart from Albi. But in less than a month's time, I would be going back, so that is what I focused on.

Tony and Sandra were due out a couple of weeks after Bill died, and they were bringing a couple of their friends with them. It was good to see them, but I had mixed emotions and tried to keep a fairly low profile. Tony said that they would be attending the memorial service, and he also said that he would give a reading. I really appreciated that.

I had not been able to contact Frank and Sheila, as they were in the middle of a cruise with Carol and Bob. The day after they were due back home, I rang them. Frank answered the phone in his usual bright and breezy manner and asked me how things were. I had to tell him my bad news and he was dumbstruck. He passed the phone to Sheila and I had to explain to her what had happened. She was genuinely upset, and I felt sorry that I had put a damper on their homecoming after a lovely holiday.

The time came for me to go home for the memorial service. Nicola had put an advertisement in the local paper so that any of Bill's friends or old workmates could attend if they wished.

Albi went into kennels while I was away; he wasn't too keen on that idea, but it was only for a week. Martin met me at the airport; I was to stay with him and his family.

It was arranged that we would have the urn interred in the local churchyard, so I had to arrange for a plot to be dug and also for a stone to be engraved.

Nicola had been in touch with the vicar with the Order of Service instructions and also details of the hymns and songs which we had chosen. I went to see a lady who had been recommended, and she promised to make flower arrangements of calla lilies for the church. Nicola, Elliot and Peter were coming to Yorkshire the day before, as were Tony and Sandra. I booked them all into a local B&B and we all met up for a meal the night before.

Martin had arranged for a buffet at the local football club for after the service. We weren't sure how many people would turn up, but we thought everything was covered. Lyn was very good and let us use her and Martin's house as a base. Her mum was taking care of baby Lewis and Ellie.

When the time for the service drew near, I began to feel nervous. However, Nicola had been earlier and made sure that the flowers and the Order of Service cards were in place in the church.

The church was packed – people I hadn't seen in years had turned up – it was all extremely emotional. The service began with Bill's favourite, 'Maggie'. Tony gave a reading of 'Crossing the Bar' by Alfred Lord Tennyson, Nicola read 'Remember Me' and did a great job, and Martin read a farewell piece to his dad. I was very proud of them all. We left the church to the sound of Frank Sinatra singing 'My Way' – very suitable for Bill. The urn was interred, and only then did I notice just how many people had actually turned up.

Afterwards, at the clubhouse, I moved around everybody. There were even old neighbours of ours and some of our old caravan friends. All the family were there – uncles and aunts and nephews and all the grandchildren – they all looked so smart. I think we did Bill proud. The buffet was lovely, but there was such a lot of food left over.

Tony and Sandra left a little early, as they were going to visit friends on the way home, and I believe they were staying overnight.

Nicola and Elliot stayed another night, and we went into Leeds the next day and bought a lovely flower arrangement with some money Frank and Sheila had sent. The icing on the cake was when we went to the churchyard the next morning and found that the memorial stone had already been put in place. The stone mason must have worked overtime to get it done before I went back to Spain. I felt pleased that everything that could be done had been done.

I returned to Spain the next day; there were no pork pies going back this time, a fact of which I was very aware. Just one more ritual which would never be repeated again for me.

It was too late to pick Albi up when I arrived home, so he would have to stay another day. The next morning, I was up bright and early to go to the kennels. Albi was so pleased to see me that it almost made it all worthwhile.

I had never driven the car in Spain, as Bill had guarded it possessively, giving me the excuse that it wasn't safe on the roads – too many idiots, he said. However, after he died, the car was there and I had to get from A to B. I was a little nervous, not about driving on the other side of the road, but more because the gears and everything were on the opposite side of the car. Tony offered to sit beside me the first couple of times, but I soon got the hang of it. I think I scared him a bit, as he kept telling me to slow down. I quite enjoyed the freedom that driving myself brought, and I didn't even feel guilty when I came back from one of my forays with a wheel trim missing. One of the first things that Bill would do when I brought his car back while we were in the UK was to check that all the wheel trims were intact.

The first Christmas that I was on my own, I went back home. I stayed at Martin's and watched the children open their presents, but for Christmas dinner I went to Flo's. I had booked a local hotel for the two of us; it was very expensive but a lovely treat. I had put Albi in kennels, again just for a week. Nicola came up to Yorkshire with Elliot on Boxing Day and we exchanged presents. It was very hectic for Nicola with all that driving, but it was hectic for me, too; there were so many people to see and places to go.

I always felt very nostalgic when I left England to return to Spain. There was no doubt about it – Bill had loved living in Spain, but it wasn't much fun, I found, when I was on my own, especially if I had any sort of problem. I decided to try to sell the house, and move back to England.

It was lovely when any of my friends were out there with me, and I did enjoy the social life, but there were times when there weren't any of my friends out and they were very long days. When Jean and Fred were out, Jean and I liked to go to the market. Sometimes we went on the bus to Benidorm or on a blanket trip, on which a bus would take you to a place where they tried to flog you pillows and blankets. We just went along for the trip and for the lunch they provided. If we went along to the market in Torrevieja, we would make a beeline for the *churros* stall. This was a kind of doughnut but in long strips, and they were freshly cooked. A bag of those delicacies was just one euro, a bargain.

The only thing about the market which was a big drawback was the fact that you had to have your purse chained to you, and even then the pickpockets would sometimes manage to part you from your money. Everyone had a tale to tell about being mugged, or knew someone who had been.

Whenever Tony and Sandra were out, it was wall-to-wall eating, but I used to get cross with Tony because he would never let me pay. One Sunday, we went out with Pat, Joe and Pat's two sisters, who were out on holiday. Sandra and Tony also went. It was a lovely lunch, and they were all very good to me.

Margaret, who lived next to Frank and Sheila, liked to come out on her own, as David was kept quite busy on the farm. She was great fun, and one evening we arranged to go to Spud Murphy's for a fish and chip supper. Margaret drove us there in her car; parking was at a premium, but we actually managed to get a spot in the small car park. When we came out after our meal, some idiot had parked his open-topped jeep right across the entrance to the car park. There were three large industrial bins on the side of the road, piled with cardboard boxes, so we filled the inside of the jeep with these boxes. A couple who were passing by couldn't do anything for laughing. Then Margaret drove her car down the pavement and managed to get out. When I told Nicola about it, she said that we would probably have an ASBO served on us. It was funny, though, and I bet the driver would think twice about parking there again.

Another time that Margaret and I went into Torrevieja, we parked on the front, along with several other cars and vans belonging to the stalls nearby. We did our shopping, had a coffee, and when we came back to the car, it was the only vehicle there – that is, apart from two police motorcyclists, who had put a barricade in place behind Margaret's car. We did an about turn and hid behind the stalls to watch them. After about fifteen minutes, one of them got a call on his walkie-talkie or whatever they had. He said something to his colleague and they both jumped on their bikes and shot off with blue lights flashing. I shot off, too, and shifted the barriers, and Margaret leapt into the driver's seat and we were away. That was a lucky escape. I think that Margaret was a bad influence on me, but we laughed all the way home.

Some months after Bill died, I was at home and Tony and Sandra were out for a couple of weeks. Jean called me and asked me if I could go with her to Charlie's as Iris wasn't well. I went running down the street with Jean, and found Iris in the downstairs bedroom. It was an awful sight – she was laid on a little bed, quite obviously dead, with one arm in the air as if she was asking to leave the room. Charlie kept saying, 'I thought she was asleep and I couldn't wake her.'

I rang for an ambulance and the lady asked whether Iris was breathing. I said that I didn't know, as I didn't want to say too much on the phone and anyway I thought that it was for them to find out. She said that an ambulance was on its way. It was all a bit too close to home for me, but I felt that I had to support Charlie. He told us that Iris had been out with him the day before; she had fallen and he had tried to get her up the steps to their house, but he'd had to manhandle her as she could hardly stand.

The ambulance men came, and Jean and I waited outside, but there was a right to-do – the ambulance men were shouting at Charlie in Spanish and waving their arms about. It seems they thought that there might have been some foul play, as Iris was very emaciated, but I don't think she used to eat very well and it was suspected that she was an alcoholic. The medics were on the phone to someone and they were gabbling away. We just watched in amazement, and Charlie kept scratching his head. Two more men in uniform came and they were pointing to the curtains in the bedroom which were hanging down.

Jean, who was taking Spanish lessons, went into the next street and brought her teacher to act as interpreter. Apparently, they were suspicious of Iris's death; it was several hours later that they took her body away. I asked Charlie whether he was going to ring his daughter in England, and he said that she would be at work and he would ring her later.

They performed an autopsy on Iris and eventually found that she died of liver failure, which didn't surprise anyone, given the amount of alcohol that she had enjoyed.

Paqui came and arranged the cremation, as she had Bill's, and we all went to the service. It was a strange affair – not very respectful somehow – and the music that they played was something outlandish like 'The Leader of the Pack'. It was all a bit weird.

For Charlie, it seemed like a new beginning. He walked with a spring in his step – probably the task of looking after Iris had weighed heavily on him in the past.

As I had a lot of time on my hands in between visitors, I spent a lot of it thinking about my and Bill's lives together, or 'raking over the past', as my aunt would have said. How different things could have been if only he had put more effort into being a good dad. All his friends, I believe, thought that he was a good mate, and to me that seemed more important to him. When I saw dads playing with their children, and even laughing with them, I felt so sorry that Bill didn't even like his children – with the emphasis on 'like'. But he did mellow (almost too late) – he mellowed not like a fine wine, but more like an old cheddar, still a bit crusty around the edges. He had really enjoyed their presence when they came to visit us in Spain, and I think he loved his grandchildren, but I do think that it was all too little too late.

He never was good at dealing with responsibility; it always seemed easier for him to put any onus on me, so that if or when things went wrong, then it was my fault. This may sound like a strange description of someone who was so domineering – he wasn't a wimp, far from it, but responsibility he preferred to shift sideways on to me. He definitely wasn't big in accepting blame.

The house had been on the market for a few weeks, but things were very quiet. I had one or two viewings, but no offers. I decided that I would go home anyway, and leave the house with an agent. Martin got me a form from the local council for a bungalow. In the meantime, I would stay with Martin and Lyn, but Albi, who I would obviously be bringing back with me, would have to stay with Nicola until I found somewhere to live.

I was intending to leave almost all the furniture in the house; obviously I would be bringing back the grandfather clock, the rocking chair and all my personal stuff. Bill's fishing tackle, all his tools and his bike would all be coming, too.

I arranged for a removal firm who worked between Spain and England to transport my stuff for me. It was going to be stored in Auntie Alma's double garage until I was settled.

Albi had to have a pet passport – he already had his jabs up to date, but whereas I could get on a flight at any time, only certain flights carried animals. It was also extremely expensive.

I had decided to pay for a bench to be placed round the pool; Bill loved that pool and I thought that it was only right that a little piece of him would be forever there. A brass plaque on it read, 'In memory of Bill – still keeping an eye on things', which I thought summed it up well.

I kept myself busy with the packing. It seemed that the whole of my life had been spent packing and unpacking. The chaps who were taking the stuff to England came to collect it, and I was left with only the things that were staying. The house was depersonalised, and I felt that already it didn't belong to me.

Tony and Sandra were out there when I was due to go; in fact, they were taking Albi and me to the airport. The night before we were due to leave, we had an evening out. There were about a dozen of us, and I got some lovely photographs, most of them showing how many bottles of wine we had drunk. We all promised to keep in touch.

The vet had given me a sedative for Albi, as he was not a good traveller in the car, let alone on a plane. Albi had to be at the airport for 9 a.m. as he would go from the freight terminal, but the flight wasn't until 1 p.m., so it was a long time for Albi to be confined in his pet carrier. I gave him his sedative and wham, down he went. We never heard a peep from him as we travelled to the airport. When we arrived at the freight terminal, a customs officer checked his papers and had a look at Albi, who was subdued but awake. He asked whether he had been sedated, and when I said that he had, the official was not at all pleased. Apparently it was no longer allowed on their airlines, as the sedative interferes with the heart rate of the animal when they are airborne.

I pointed out that we were not flying until 1 p.m. and that by then the effects would almost have worn off. Obviously the vet hadn't known of this ruling or he wouldn't have prescribed the sedative in the first place. The official accepted my explanation and we left Albi with him. The next time I would see him would be in good old Blighty.

Tony drove me to the main terminal and watched as I checked in. I didn't want them to wait with me, as I felt emotional enough as it was. I was upset to say goodbye, as they were very good friends to me and to Bill; in fact, I still look on them as good friends, and we keep in touch.

It was surprising how quickly the time went. I had some lunch and a look around the shops and read the paper, and then it was time to board. Arriving at Gatwick, I found chaos – it was the day of the London bombings, so there were long queues at the enquiry desk, with travellers wanting to find alternative routes into London. I just wanted to know where to pick Albi up, but I had to join the queue of enquirers. I was told that I would have to go to the freight terminal, and I would need a cab to get there. I was panicking, as Nicola and Elliot were meeting me at the airport. I only had a fifty-pence piece in English money, and hoped that it would be enough to get hold of Nicola on her mobile. I managed to get hold of her and she told me to stay where I was, and she would come and get me. Within five minutes, Nicola and Elliot appeared in the doorway of the airport, and we set off to track down Albi.

It was quite some distance away, and I would never have got there if I hadn't had Nicola. I was getting a bit panicky, as I couldn't begin to know what state Albi would be in. We arrived at the reception desk and showed our documentation, and the lady said that she would fetch him. She asked us whether he had been sedated and I had to admit that he had – she said I was very lucky, as they could have refused to carry him. They had had to change his bedding, as it was soaking wet, and they had put shredded paper in the bottom of his pet carrier. He was so pleased to see me that he went bonkers; I think he thought that he had been abandoned. We put him on the lead and let him have a little walk around the car park to stretch his legs, and he was soon as good as new. It wasn't too long a journey to Nicola's house; he was in for a good spoiling.

The very first evening that I was home, Martin rang to say that I had been offered a council bungalow. It was in a little village I didn't know much about, but beggars can't be choosers. Martin was picking the keys up the next day and going to have a look at it on my behalf. I couldn't believe it, even if it only saw me through until I got on my feet. It also meant that I wouldn't have to live with Martin and Lyn, which would be better for them. Martin reported back that the bungalow wasn't bad – although it had been rewired throughout, so needed decorating everywhere. There was a small front garden but no fence, and the workmen had left it in a hell of a state. The council agreed that I could have it for a week before paying rent. I told Martin to accept it on my behalf, and asked him whether he could put up some fencing to keep Albi in. The problem was that for the next two weeks Martin and Lyn were going to France, so it looked as though I was going to be on my own.

I decided to leave Albi with Nicola and go up to Yorkshire. If I only managed to decorate and lay the carpets, then I could fetch Albi home.

I stayed at Martin's while they were in France, but I did find it very hard going working on my new house, as every room had woodchip on, which had been painted over and over again. It was damned hard work stripping every room. Ann lent me her car, as the village where I was to live was in the back of beyond, and I needed to buy paint and wallpaper and also choose carpets. Hollie and Laura came for a couple of days and gave me a hand with the stripping. I was desperate to make it habitable as quickly as possible.

The previous occupants had even ripped the curtain rails down, so I had to screw some new ones up. When Martin came home and had a look at what I had done, he told me that one of the curtain rails was upside down. Oh well! But the painting and papering were done to my specifications, and if they didn't suit anybody – well, tough. I even managed to put a bathroom cabinet up, and used a spirit level. Bill would have been proud of me.

I didn't think it looked bad at all when it was done. I had ordered carpets and bought the essentials to see me through until I got my bearings. Ann's ex-husband borrowed a van from work and brought my things from Aunty Alma's garage to the bungalow. The little place was beginning to look like a home, and the next stop was to go and bring Albi home. I went down on the train and stayed a couple of days, and then Elliot's dad drove me up to Yorkshire with Albi, along with all the stuff I had left with Nicola.

Albi was so pleased to be in his own place, and soon staked his claim to his favourite spot in the lounge. He also loved the garden and the freedom.

Martin found me a car which had a few years on it but was in fairly good nick. The car was essential, as I had to drive for every little thing that I needed. There were no facilities in the village – not even a shop, just a pub.

I resumed my trips with Flo at least once a week; we would go out for lunch, and then call at the supermarket to stock up.

The ladies whom I had worked with at the bacon factory met up twice a year for a meal and a natter, so I was getting back into the swing of things slowly. I did miss my friends in Spain, although they phoned regularly and wrote with news now and again.

Pat and Joe decided to sell their house in Spain, so there were going to be new faces in our street. I heard from my agent that someone had put in an offer for my property in Spain, and I decided to accept it. I would have to go out there some time in the future to sign it over, so it looked like a trip to the kennels again for Albi.

When the time came for me to go and hand over the house, I had very mixed feelings. It would be a relief not to have the responsibility of the place, but at the same time, it would be a final severing with the link in Spain with Bill. There was quite a bit of running about to do – to the solicitor, to the bank, and having a final look around the property. I didn't stay in Spain longer than I had to, as it was not a holiday.

I had been back home for a year when what would have been our golden wedding anniversary came around. I went to the churchyard and took some yellow roses for Bill's grave, and Ann turned up with a bottle of bubbly. Just as we were about to toast Bill, Nicola and Elliot came as well, so we had more bubbly.

I bought myself a static caravan on the coast, as a kind of bolt-hole, as I did not enjoy living in the bungalow. I must admit that I loved escaping to the caravan. I had some friends already living on the same site. It was also quite near to the site where Bill and I had had a caravan some years ago, so I sometimes popped over to look up old friends.

As the van was quite a journey from where I lived, I thought it wise to get a more reliable car, so I bought one just twelve months old. I have also managed to pick up a speeding ticket for the first time in thirty-five years of driving, so instead of slowing down I seem to be speeding up!

I have had several invitations from my friends in Spain to go out for a break. For the first year, I didn't feel able to do it, but a few months ago I went to stay with Margaret for a week. I did enjoy it, although I think that I put on half a stone in weight. Margaret did me a full English breakfast, followed by a full English dinner and a full English tea! But it was lovely seeing most of my friends, and we caught up on all the news. One evening, nine of us went out for a meal – even Charlie went. I went to visit Bill's bench at the pool and buffed up his plaque a bit. I do miss everybody, and I am looking forward to going out there again this year.

As I have grown more elderly, I find I have suffered a personality change. I had always thought that I was fairly compliant, but now I should audition for *Grumpy Old Women*. I have an opinion on everything from global warming to the abolition of the House of Lords to devolution. And woe betide a cold caller if they happen to ring (and they always do) when I am enjoying my afternoon tea. Road rage, trolley rage and queue jumping – don't even go there. Add all this to the points on my driving licence, and I begin to wonder whether I have a problem. I do admire the senior ladies who are prepared to go to prison rather than pay the extortionate increases in their council tax. I can feel my muscles flexing as I write; perhaps it's all in the spinach that I eat – or it could be the medication.

So – that's about where I am right now. Will I go on my travels again? Probably. Will I move house again? More than likely. But as long as I have the love of my kids, and they stay close to each other, I don't ask for anything more.

900762

Printed in Great Britain by
Amazon.co.uk, Ltd.,
Marston Gate.